Andrew Carnegie

Insight and Analysis into the Life of a True Entrepreneur, Industrialist, and Philanthropist

Andrew Carnegie

Insight and Analysis into the Life of a True Entrepreneur, Industrialist, and Philanthropist

JR MacGregor

Andrew Carnegie – Insight and Analysis into the Life of a True Entrepreneur, Industrialist, and Philanthropist

Published by CAC Publishing LLC.

ISBN 978-1-950010-27-1 paperback

ISBN 978-1-950010-26-4 eBook

Contents

Introduction

Andrew Carnegie was born November 25, 1835, in the attic of his parents' one-story house, located on the corner of Moodie Street and Priory Lane in Dunfermline, Scotland.

His father, William Carnegie, was a damask weaver, who supported the family by weaving fabric and selling it in the neighborhood.

The Carnegies, from Grandpa Carnegie all the way down to little Andrew, were well known in this little Scottish town that dates back to 1071 when Malcolm III reigned.

It was Malcolm's queen, Margaret, who commissioned the construction of the abbey that Carnegie would spend hours looking at when he was six years old.

Carnegie's mother, Margaret, was a strong woman who believed that it was her place to care for her husband and children. Even when she had to mend shoes for extra income, she would do it after all her chores were done and her boys were fed and put to bed.

Andrew Carnegie deeply admired and cherished his parents and learned from them the value of family and the power of hard work.

His parents did everything they could in an economy that was dwindling and an age that was rapidly changing.

Chapter 1 Dunfermline

Dunfermline was the center of the Scottish linen industry during Andrew Carnegie's childhood. It is located approximately twenty miles northwest of Edinburgh, the capital of Scotland.

It was a small town measuring no more than nine miles from north to south and six miles from east to west. At the time of Carnegie's childhood, the town had about three thousand homes, which were laid out in orderly fashion with the abbey and the castle ruins in the center where the two main roads crossed. The castle ruins are what is left of King Malcolm's court.

From the city's center crossroads, all other streets and lanes branched out to checker the city's cottages and businesses.

It is important to note that before the Industrial Revolution the commercial structure across Britain consisted primarily of agrarian and cottage industries where everyone worked on individual farms and in their cottages.

Being known for its high-quality linen, the city was centered around the marketplace, where merchants would hawk their wares. At its height, the Dunfermline marketplace had more than three thousand high-quality handlooms on sale in a vibrant and prosperous atmosphere. After buying up their supply of woven fabric and fancy damask from various individual weavers in town, merchants would offer them for sale in the marketplace.

The linen was in such high demand that merchants would come from other towns and cities in the fiefdom and surrounding parishes to take stock and then travel south to England or across the channel into France in search of customers.

Andrew's father was one of these high-quality and sought-after weavers. The handlooms that William Carnegie produced were in high demand and popular with merchants. William only had to stay at home and spend his time weaving, and merchants were almost beating down his door for more supply.

Then came a seismic event that shook the world. It was a confluence of agriculture and industry when the British started to take their supply of cotton from India and had it shipped to Manchester.

Manchester was the industrial world's first success story. It was driven by mechanization and the first city to build factories that dominated the textile industry.

Thanks to Richard Arkwright's first textile mill in 1781, the price of woven fabric had started to fall, forcing other textile merchants keep up with the falling prices and, in turn, demanding a cheaper process from the weavers.

This was the first wave of problems in the handloom industry. The second wave came when factories began springing up outside

Dunfermline and were able to produce linen at cheaper prices.

Besides the regular linen looms that were in these mechanized textile mills, they began to outfit some of them with the mechanical addition that could handle damask weaving, which was a specialization and not something the regular mills could handle.

To be able to do damask looms for specialty linen used in table cloths and expensive clothing, they had to attach another invention that came from France—the Jacquard machine.

That came soon after, and by 1847, the demand for William Carnegie's handlooms had almost vanished. Merchants who had beaten down his doors for supply were now taking their linen from the mills that were just outside the town.

It was not just the Carnegie household that came under the heel of industrialization; most of Dunfermline felt the smack of progress.

Chapter 2 Family in Scotland

Carnegie was surrounded by radicals. His father and relatives were all politically involved and quite vocal. His Uncle Bailie Morrison was once arrested for holding a political meeting that had been forbidden as unlawful assembly. That type of law was common in those days to prevent uprisings and revolts. If you couldn't congregate, you couldn't conspire.

The meeting had taken place some distance away from Dunfermline, and Carnegie's uncle was brought into the city after being arrested. The townspeople planned to free him, but that would have caused a riot. The mayor of Dunfermline, however, convinced him to send the would-be protestors away. His word dispersed his fellow radicals, and they returned to their homes in peace.

As a clan, the Carnegies were radical, strong-minded, and clear-eyed, but they were not troublemakers.

Carnegie came from a land where each person worked for their own well-being. There was no talk of slaves in Dunfermline, and so when thrust into the debate of slavery some years later in the United States, he didn't see it as a righteous issue. Given his vocal ancestry, like his uncles and father before him, he was vocal about politics in the U.S. as well. This combination of opinion and loquaciousness fueled his political preference.

damask

Carnegie was a strong supporter of antislavery, and when the Republican party had its first meeting on February 22, 1856, Carnegie supported the abolition of slavery. Although just a few months short of being able to vote, he supported Lincoln with full vigor and principle.

Strong opinions notwithstanding, the matter at hand in old-world Scotland was still about the daily necessities of living.

As the despair among the hand weavers deepened, the Carnegies sunk with it. They had to relocate, move into smaller dwellings, and minimize their expenses. Their circumstances became tight.

The once lucrative career of a damask weaver no longer yielded much. It was made worse by the existence of a middleman—the merchants—who were getting it cheap from the mills and then adding their markup before selling it to the end consumer.

The only way William Carnegie could keep up was to go directly to the customer himself. There was little demand for the higher priced handlooms, so the entire family had to live on little to nothing.

It was a difficult time, as William had to make the fabric and then spend time going from door to door, town to town trying to make a sale. This went on for some time, and to make ends meet, Margaret started selling groceries from the house. She also put up a sign and started mending shoes for neighbors.

For the better part of Carnegie's early childhood, he did not attend formal school. His parents had decided that they would not send him until he asked to go. He never asked.

After some time, however, they began to worry. They convinced a Mr. Martin, the headmaster of a nearby school, to give their son a nudge. Mr. Martin took Carnegie out for a field trip with the other children in the school, and Carnegie soon asked his parents to send him to school.

He loved school so much that he would get upset if he was late or couldn't go. Since he had to fetch water from the neighborhood well, he had to do that first before going to school, which sometimes delayed him.

When Carnegie reached the well in a rush to get back to school, he would meet several older ladies waiting to collect their water. While he waited, he had the tendency to argue with them, which earned him the moniker of "awfu' laddie." Mr. Martin, however, understood the reasons whenever Carnegie showed up late.

Carnegie admired Mr. Martin and was deeply grateful to him. He saw the headmaster as a good person and was glad to attend school. Due to his fondness of Mr. Martin, he was bullied and given the nickname, "Martin's pet," which bullies shouted as he walked the streets. He did not fully understand its meaning, so he didn't respond. A strategy that would serve him in his adult life—when faced with a bully—was never engage.

Carnegie had to stop at the store after school to pick up supplies so that his mother could sell them in her little grocery store. Shopkeepers soon got to know him and liked this personable young man. Once they knew he was fairly good with numbers, they got him to help with their accounts. From such unexpected circumstances, Carnegie was suddenly exposed to the world of business and commerce.

As children, Carnegie and his cousin, George Lauder, whose nickname was "Dod," were taught

Scottish history and other world events by their Uncle Lauder.

One of the strategies their uncle used was to tell the boys to imagine the subject of their lesson to be somewhere in the room doing what they were known for.

So, for Carnegie, he imagined King John reciting the *Magna Carta* while sitting on the Carnegie mantelpiece. It made him giggle, but it also made him remember.

Carnegie also learned about King Robert the Bruce and Wallace, a Scottish hero. He and his cousin used to carry out plays and recite dialogue in the play.

Whenever Carnegie or his cousin had to say the word, "hell," they usually omitted it and filled the blank space with a guttural sound, which caused their audience to laugh. They were not accustomed to swearing, and uttering "hell" in the Carnegie household was swearing. Carnegie's uncle let him off the hook, however, and allowed the boys to say the word without fear of punishment. Soon, they were saying it quite often with ease.

Carnegie's favorite place in Dunfermline was the Dunfermline Abbey, which was not very far from his home.

Whenever Carnegie was about to return home from the house of his Uncle Lauder and Dod, he was asked by his uncle which path he was going to take. There were two paths. One was brightly lit and much more welcoming than the second path, which was by the dark abbey in the churchyard. Carnegie was always tempted to take the brightly lit path, but thinking about what Wallace might do, he never once took the comfortable path. He always stuck to the dark abbey.

While he strode through the abbey, he whistled to keep up his courage and hide from his fears. He also thought of what William Wallace would do if he encountered an enemy, be he natural or not.

William Carnegie was striving hard at this time to make enough money to move back into a larger house, and eventually he was able to pull it off. Carnegie's father's looms occupied the ground floor, and the family resided upstairs.

It was not long after this that the family was all gathered in the upstairs area and looking over a map of a country called America. It was Carnegie's earliest memory of hearing about this strange and mythical place.

In the upstairs residence, the adults had spread the map on the dining table and were trying to find a place called Pittsburgh. Soon thereafter, Aunt Aitken set off for this city.

The brief upswing they had in their fortunes didn't last long. William was soon struggling to sell linen, and the family started to struggle too.

This time they didn't see any way out of it that would be lasting. It was clear that handlooms were a thing of the past, and that mechanization of the textile industry had changed things forever.

The only option they had was to try for a new beginning and follow in the footsteps of Aunt Aitken.

This is what they decided to do. As long as they could save enough to make passage, they would throw their destiny to the winds of the North Atlantic. They made contact with a Mrs. Henderson, an old friend of Margaret Carnegie, who had settled in Pittsburgh.

Mrs. Henderson said she would welcome them, and the Carnegie family began accumulating the necessary money to set sail. When the time finally came to leave the house in Dunfermline, the Carnegie family boarded the carriage on the coal line and headed for the port. As the carriage rumbled away, Carnegie watched Dunfermline disappear from the window. The last thing he saw were the towers of his favorite abbey. His young eyes welled up with tears, but he managed to control himself and swore that he would return someday.

This departure from Dunfermline was difficult for young Andrew, but he stood fast. He bit lip so hard that it bled and said to himself, "No matter, keep cool; you must go on."

When the family was about to board the ship to New York, Carnegie found that he could not let go of his Uncle Lauder. His mind commanded that he leave, but his heart clung to his uncle. For his part, Uncle Lauder could not hold back his tears or unlock his arms from around his favorite nephew.

In the end, one of the sailors intervened to help Margaret with her son and hoisted Carnegie up onto the ship. That sailor later remarked that it was the saddest parting he had ever seen—and he had seen quite a few.

Carnegie's heavy heart followed him as the ship weighed anchor and set sail out of the harbor. As the ship slipped over the horizon and the land behind them was no longer in sight, the thrill of new beginnings and the prospect of being in a ship distracted him into laughter and joy.

Carnegie enjoyed the trip aboard the *Wiscasset*. He befriended the crew and explored various parts of the ship. This friendship only deepened over the course of the voyage, and by the time they disembarked in New York, Carnegie was crestfallen to leave his new friends.

After clearing immigration and health inspections, Carnegie had his first taste of New York. He was overwhelmed by the chaos and rush of the city.

To get to Pittsburgh, Carnegie's father was advised to go through Buffalo. To do that, they needed to take the Erie Canal to Lake Erie and then up to Beaver before reaching their destination.

This journey lasted three weeks, but Carnegie was happy with the trip. The only thing that was rather uncomfortable was the night spent on the ferry at Beaver. They were waiting for the steamer to arrive so that they would be transported on the Ohio River up to Pittsburgh. That night was truly hellish, for the family faced mosquitos for the first time. They were badly bitten, yet Carnegie was still able to sleep soundly. The night had been so severe that his mother and father looked ghastly from the swelling the following morning.

Once the Carnegies arrived in Pittsburgh, Mrs. Henderson opened her house to them, where she provided lodging free of charge. Uncle Lauder's brother, Hogan, was also in Pittsburgh, and he was a weaver as well. He had a small shop in Pittsburgh, which he soon quit, and William was more than happy to take over and get right back to weaving.

The money he earned, however, was not sufficient to provide for the family. By this time, the problem he had faced in Dunfermline was beginning to rear its ugly head across the

Atlantic as well. Machines were already doing the sewing, and nobody wanted to employ a weaver to sew their items. Carnegie's father was forced to sew his own fabrics and then go door to door to try to sell what he had made. This was not at all sufficient, and Carnegie's mother again started mending shoes.

Margaret was well versed in mending shoes because she used to do it as a young girl for extra pocket money to buy pins for little girls to wear in their hair. Now she was doing it to protect her family.

The Carnegie family had no servants, and Carnegie's mother was forced to do all the cleaning and cooking. When she finally had a short interval of time, Carnegie's younger brother, Thomas, would sit on her lap and thread needles. While he did so, his mother would recite Scottish poetry. At midnight, she would be seen mending shoes.

Carnegie was thirteen years old when the family began this new life in Pittsburgh. He was aware of the difficulties that his parents were facing and wanted to help.

Just after they moved to Pittsburgh, Uncle Hogan suggested to Margaret that Andrew could make some money selling knickknacks at the wharf. When he suggested this, Margaret was sewing but found the energy to jump up and begin screaming at him. She said, "What! my son a peddler and among rough men upon the wharves! I would rather throw him into the Allegheny River. Leave me!" and pointed to the door.

Margaret wanted more for her sons. That much was clear. She did not want them to become just anyone who sold goods at the wharves. She wanted her children to become something great.

It was apparent to Carnegie's father that his current line of work was not going to be enough. So, he entered the cotton business under one Mr. Blackstock, a fellow Scotsman.

It was an all-hands-on-deck situation. Their financial situation was dire and compounded and complicated because they were in a new land. William continued working at the cotton business, and Margaret continued with her shoe mending. Andrew's younger brother was still too young to get a job, but Andrew was able to find work in the cotton business too.

He was hired as a bobbin boy at a textile mill and paid the sum of $1.20 a week. He hated the job but felt proud that he was helping his family. He loved that he was no longer merely a consumer but part of the solution.

Despite his pride, the job was difficult. He and his father had to rise very early in the morning and reach the factory before daylight to start work. They would only have a very short break for lunch, and then they would get back home long after dark.

After spending some time at this work and not liking it at all, fate dealt him a break when he was able to land a job that paid more.

This next job was under one Mr. John Hay, who manufactured bobbins. Carnegie's job was to manage the boilers at the bobbin factory. It turned out that he despised this job even more than the last one. He was paid $2 a week and spent his time managing the steam gauges. He was in constant fear that the steam might be too low and that there would be not enough power for the workers above. He was also in constant fear that the steam would be too high and that the boiler would explode.

He never mentioned these difficulties to his parents, though, and just did the work and contributed to his family.

All the while he kept his ear out for a better job— one that would be easier to do and pay more. He never complained. He just wanted better,

And he got what he wished for. Carnegie's next job was as a telegram delivery boy. This job had been offered to him by a Mr. Brooks. Carnegie's mother supported the idea, but this time his father opposed it. He thought Carnegie was too young and small in size to be able to protect himself. What if he needed to send a telegram in the dead of night? Could he defend himself?

Soon, however, Carnegie's father relented but said he would follow his son to meet Mr. Brooks. Andrew told his father, however, that he could follow him only to the telegraph office.

So, when Carnegie and his father reached the office, his father waited outside, and Andrew entered to meet Mr. Brooks. His interview was successful, and when Mr. Brooks asked when he could start, he said that he would start now if he could. So began the life of Andrew Carnegie as a telegram delivery boy.

Chapter 3 Telegram

After having been hired as a telegram delivery boy, Carnegie had to learn the layout of the city so that he could deliver the telegrams to the right houses. He soon memorized the different places and was able to deliver the messages with ease.

Shortly after he started work, another boy was hired to deliver telegrams in the same area as Carnegie. His name was David McCargo, and he was a fellow Scotsman. Later, Carnegie was asked to find another boy who could be hired to deliver telegrams. Without a second thought, Carnegie recommended Robert Pitcairn, who was also a countryman. The three grew to be good friends and had monikers for each other. Andrew was Andy, David was Davy, and Robert was Bob.

During Carnegie's tenure, the telegram delivery business paid a bonus of ten cents to the delivery boy if he delivered a message to someplace farther away than usual.

These bonuses were highly sought after, and the telegram delivery boys began to argue over who was to deliver the messages. It was sometimes the case that some boys had delivered messages assigned to someone else. It had become a real problem.

Carnegie had an idea and soon decided that the delivery boys would combine their earnings. Since it was his idea, the boys decided that Carnegie would manage the money.

Unlike Carnegie, the other boys did not think about saving their money but spent every penny lavishly at the confectionery shop nearby—and they would do it on credit.
Carnegie had to inform the confectioner that he was not going to pay for what the boys spent if they spent more than their share.

Robert Pitcairn was the worst spender of all. He kept racking up his bill at the confectioners.

When Carnegie confronted him about it, he said that monsters lived inside him, and that they chewed on his insides until he fed them.

The pay each month was $11.25. Carnegie was always the first to be paid. All the boys would stand in a line, and the man paying them would walk down that line, paying all the boys, and Carnegie, being first in line, was paid first.

Then came the day when things changed. All the boys had lined up as usual with Carnegie at the front of the line, but when the time came, he was looked over and not paid. Mr. Glass simply paid all the other boys. Carnegie was deeply worried. He felt that he had been dismissed. His greatest worry was the repercussions this would have on his family.

After all the boys had been paid and left the room, Mr. Glass took Carnegie behind the counter and told him that he was worth more than any of the other boys. His salary was raised to $13.50 a month.

Carnegie took the money, and without even saying "Thank you" or anything else for that matter, started walking home. This time, however, he found himself going a little faster than usual. When he reached home, he did not speak of his raise and only gave his mother the usual $11.25. That night, however, when Carnegie and his younger brother, Thomas, were in bed, Carnegie went to his brother and showed him the remaining $2.25. Even Tom, as young as he was, could understand the situation, and Carnegie explained to him how the two of them would go into business together and start the firm of Carnegie Brothers. This money was really very important to Carnegie.

At breakfast the next morning, Carnegie placed the $2.25 on the table. His parents were speechless, and it took them a moment to realize what it really meant. Carnegie's mother was immensely happy, and his father was immensely proud. The extra money meant that Carnegie was good at his job and worthy of being paid more.

Although working as a telegram delivery boy had many benefits, Carnegie did not like that he never had time to read his books. His end time was different every day. He might be let off at 6:00 p.m. one day but at 11:00 p.m. the next. Soon, however, to Carnegie's delight, Colonel James Henderson opened his library of four hundred books to all the working boys. The question then was whether or not a telegram delivery boy would be able to borrow books from the library. Carnegie thus wrote a letter to the press stating that although he and his fellow telegram delivery boys did not work with their hands, some of them had, and they should be allowed to visit the library. Colonel Henderson then widened the scope of classification for those who entered his library.

The boys who visited the library would go in one Saturday, borrow a book, and then exchange that book for another one the following Saturday.

Carnegie was delighted to have a chance to read books. During his short breaks, he would spend his time reading the book he had borrowed from the library and not put it down until it was time to get back to work.

Carnegie's path to being the assistant operator started when he entered the telegram business, but it started directly when he began meddling in the operator's office. One operator, who was all too lazy, was more than happy to let Carnegie do the work. Later, when a telegram operator in Greensburg said that he had to go off for some time, Carnegie was sent to work as acting operator until he returned. One stormy night, Carnegie sat close to the machine at all times, not wanting to turn off the connection. At one point, he got a little too close to the keys of the machine and was thrown off his stool after being electrocuted by lightning that had struck just when Carnegie was near the machine. He was seen as being cautious and able to complete his duties to the satisfaction of those who held higher office. Later, Mr. Reid, who was the superintendent of the line, needed an assistant operator, and Mr. Brooks recommended Carnegie for the position. Mr. Reid was more than willing to accept Carnegie as long as Mr. Brooks considered him up to the task. Carnegie then became an assistant operator and paid the handsome sum of $1 for every day he worked, which amounted to $25 a month.

The Pittsburgh newspapers always sent reporters to take down the letters of the press. After a time, one man was put in charge of this and asked if perhaps the newspapers could be duplicated several times. Carnegie was the one to do it, and for this job he was paid $1 a week, raising his monthly earnings to $30.

After some time, Carnegie wrote all his telegrams by sound and no longer used traditional print. Finding someone who could take down telegrams by sound was not normal. Many people visited the office simply to watch how it was done. Carnegie had attracted so much attention from this work that when a flood destroyed the telegram communication lines between Steubenville and Wheeling, which were twenty-five miles away from each other, Carnegie was sent to Steubenville to take in all that was going on between the East and the West. At hourly intervals, Carnegie was to send dispatches to Wheeling. These were transported in small boats. Wheeling would then send out more dispatches back to Steubenville. In this way, telegraph communication between the East and the West as far as Pittsburgh was concerned continued to work smoothly.

While Carnegie was in Steubenville, he received word that his father was traveling to Cincinnati and then to Wheeling to sell his tablecloths. Carnegie went to wait for the boat to meet his father. The boat did not arrive until late evening, and Carnegie did not like his father riding as a deck passenger. He had not wanted to pay the hefty expense of traveling as a cabin passenger. Carnegie said to him that he and his mother would soon be riding in their carriage. Carnegie's father, being Scotch, rarely praised his son or anyone else for that matter. Now, however, he was not able to hold back and told him, "Andra, I am proud of you." He then said goodnight and told Carnegie to go back to his office. Andrew was deeply pleased by his father's words.

Shortly afterward, Carnegie's father passed away. Carnegie himself has described his father to be the personification of kindness itself. Andrew admired his father, and although he, his brother, and his mother all loved him, they had no time to sit and sob. They had to tend to work to keep the household alive.

A certain David McCandless, however, who was a member of the Swedenborgian Society, offered to assist the Carnegie family with money. Carnegie's mother, however, refused the aid. They didn't need it. Despite not needing his help, he had earned a place in their hearts.

Carnegie soon met a man by the name of Thomas A. Scott, who would bring him back to work for the Pennsylvania Railroad Company, which had only come into existence in 1846, just seven years before he began his job in the company. Carnegie began working at the Pennsylvania Railroad Company as Mr. Scott's secretary. Mr. Scott had actually asked if he could hire Carnegie, but his assistant had replied that he could not for he was already an operator. Carnegie, however, wanted more than just sitting in an office writing telegrams all day. He accepted the job and began work on February 1, 1853. He would eventually work his way up to become a division superintendent of the Pennsylvania Railroad Company.

Chapter 4 Railroad

The railroad industry began in 1812 when Colonel John Stevens invented the first locomotive. It was exactly like a horse carriage but was powered by a steam engine.

Stevens also built the railway for the locomotive to travel on. He was later called the Father of American Railroads. Stevens had planned to build the New Jersey Railroad Company, but his plans never came to life.

In 1827, the Baltimore and Ohio Railroad, which is the oldest railroad company in the United States, created the first common carrier railroad, which carried both freight and passenger trains. Three years after the Baltimore and Ohio Railroad came into existence, the first mechanical train was invented and thus began the modern age of the railroad industry.

Many small railroad companies emerged several years later and created their own railway operations. After a few decades, some nine thousand miles of track was spread across the country.

Other railroad companies soon appeared. The New York Central Railroad Company, for instance, resulted from the merger of twelve small railway lines, while the Illinois Railroad Company's growth was boosted by the rights it had been given by the federal government. As for the Pennsylvania Railroad Company, it did not come into existence until late in 1846. When it did come about and became better known, its division superintendent was none other than Andrew Carnegie.

Carnegie began working at the Pennsylvania Railroad Company in 1853, eight years before the first shots were fired at Fort Sumter.

In the wake of Abraham Lincoln's election to the presidency in 1861, he signed the Railroad Act of 1862, which served as the impetus for the construction of the first transcontinental railroad.

The Union Pacific began building on the East Coast, while the Central Pacific began construction in the West. It took seven years for construction to make its way inland, and on May 10, 1869, the two railroads met at Promontory Point, Utah.
It was there that the Golden Spike, also known  as the Last Spike, was thrust into the ground, marking the completion of the first transcontinental railroad.

During the Civil War, expansion of the railroad industry reduced, while use of the railroads increased.

Smaller railroad companies began to disappear after the Civil War, and larger companies came into existence. By 1917, more than 250,000 miles of track was spread across the United States.

At first, Carnegie did not like his job at the railroad company. The problem had nothing to do with the work he did but was more about the people he had to rub shoulders with. Carnegie was not the rough and tumble kind of teenager. He had grown up surrounded by well-mannered people, and he behaved the same way.

His mother, who was his living role model, was well-mannered and cultured. She was a humble, churchgoing lady of polished upbringing. This is what he was used to.

fish out of water

Those who worked in the rail industry, however, such as firemen, engineers, and others, were rather gruff characters. They chewed tobacco and often cursed. It was a mind-wrecking experience for him, and Carnegie's only solace was that after work he could return to the comfort of his home, where all was good and pure.

Sometime early in his career, he was sent by Mr. Scott to Altoona to collect the checks and payrolls that were issued every month. The trip to Altoona was not going to be made over the Allegheny Mountains but rather across the plains. This made the trip rather enjoyable for Carnegie. In Altoona, he met with the general superintendent of the Pennsylvania Railroad Company, a Mr. Lombaert. At the time, Mr. Lombaert's secretary was Robert Pitcairn (Bob with the voracious appetite for confectionary), whom Carnegie had recommended for the post. David McCargo (Davy, who was also one of the delivery boys) was also at the Pennsylvania Railroad Company, and thus the three friends were in the same line of work.

The evening before Carnegie headed back to Pittsburgh with the checks and payrolls Mr. Lombaert asked him to tea much to Carnegie's surprise. Carnegie accepted his invitation with trepidation and anxiously waited for the time. Mrs. Lombaert, his host for the evening, was very kind when he arrived at the Lombaert home. He was introduced to Mrs. Lombaert with the words, "This is Mr. Scott's 'Andy'." Carnegie felt rather proud to be seen as belonging to Mr. Scott.

Carnegie set off to return to Pittsburgh the next morning with the checks and payroll tucked under his waistcoat, which he thought was a safe place. Since Carnegie rather liked trains, on his ride back to Pittsburgh, he spent his time in the engine room. After some time, he discovered that the checks and payroll were gone.

They had fallen onto the tracks somewhere over the last few miles. Thinking quickly and unhesitatingly, he asked the driver to back up the engine until they found it. Thankfully, the driver consented. While the train chugged in reverse, Carnegie scanned the area for his lost package. After some time, he spotted it along the banks of a river. He then held onto it the rest of the way back to Pittsburgh.

The fireman and engineer were the only ones who knew about the mishap, and Carnegie made them promise not to say a word of it to anyone. This "little" mishap really could have cost Carnegie his job.

It was during his time with the railroad that he became interested in politics. It was also a tumultuous time in the history of the nation.

As he became more certain of himself and understood the workings of the railroad business, one could see the metamorphosis that altered his vision and his presence.

As division superintendent, among other duties, Mr. Scott had to attend to wrecks and mishaps on the company's lines. He was the only person with the authority to send telegraphic orders to trains that operated under his jurisdiction.
His other duties as division superintendent took him away the office rather often. Sometimes his absence was caused by a wreck somewhere or perhaps other company business.

One morning Carnegie found that Mr. Scott was not in the office. He was away tending to an accident, which had caused the trains to stop in certain places, but then there was another accident in another part of the line that Mr. Scott didn't know about since he was away from the office. The trains along those lines were being guided by a flagman.

Carnegie then resolved to solve the matter by himself. To do that, he had to break the rules of access to the telegraph. He knew that if his plan failed it would mean the end of his job and perhaps even have criminal consequences. He also knew, however, that he could pull it off. He was confident.

Carnegie then started to look at where all there trains were and what problems they were facing. Keeping in mind the accident that was being handled by Mr. Scott, he made sure not to direct any trains toward that line and sorted the other trains toward their destinations with slight detours.

He then wrote out all the telegraphic orders under the name of Thomas A. Scott. Once all the orders were dispatched, the drivers and engineers as well as the flagmen complied and began to do as Carnegie had instructed.

Within a few hours, all the trains were on their way and moving smoothly. None of the lines had any more delays, and all went well.

After Mr. Scott returned to the office, he inquired about how things were going. Carnegie told him that all was fine. He then told him what had happened while he was away. Mr. Scott began to write on a piece of paper. Carnegie also told him the current locations of all the different trains and mentioned the reports that came from the different stations the trains passed through.

Mr. Scott said nothing but simply stared at the daring young Scotsman. He then left Carnegie's desk and retired to his own. He said nothing of approval or reproach. If the consequences were favorable, then all was well, but if they were disastrous, the responsibility was Carnegie's alone.

Carnegie did not feel very easy about what he had done until that evening. Mr. Scott had talked with the head of the freight agency, who was at the time a Mr. Franciscus. Mr. Scott told him what Carnegie had done, and when Mr. Franciscus asked whether or not everything went well, Mr. Scott replied that Carnegie had done all right. Carnegie was satisfied with this outcome and promised never to give telegraph orders again unless he was given the proper authority to do so. That promise was unnecessary because from then on Carnegie was trusted to manage the fleet and send out orders.

This aspect of Carnegie's character was inherent. He was a well-mannered child, but he had a level of tenacity that allowed him to make bold moves and take unconventional steps. Just this incident alone and the one where he dropped the payroll on the tracks should give an astute observer insight into the mind of this future titan of industry.

The core of Carnegie's ability can be divided into three layers. On the one hand, he had a different way of assessing risk. Not everyone can do this since assessment of risk is a skill that you have to work hard to develop if it is not something that comes naturally to you.

The second layer was his ability to minimize that risk before assuming it. If you are not observant and do not take steps to mitigate much of the risk, then you are taking on the risk at a higher level than you need to. Carnegie instinctively knew what needed to be done because he had been observing the way operations at the office were conducted, and this gave him the added skill set to solve a problem when it presented itself.

The Chinese logogram for "crisis" is interesting. It defines this moment perfectly. It is the combination of two other words—danger and opportunity. In Carnegie's case, that track crisis

Chinese for Crisis

danger

opportunity

that he could have easily washed his hands of turned out to be an opportunity.

The third layer requires the active willingness to do something or to take on the crisis and convert it to an opportunity. If you look at this instance, the crisis was not even Carnegie's doing or his responsibility to fix. No one would have said anything to him for not lifting a finger, but he seized the opportunity, and because he had been observant in the past, he was successful.

When John Edgar Thomson, a colleague of Mr. Scott, visited the office, he addressed Carnegie as "Scott's Andy." Carnegie thought that one needs to do something beyond what he is expected to do to be noticed by those above him. That is how one opens doors to higher places.

As an example, when Mr. Scott was once away, Carnegie had been appointed to take care of things while he was gone. At the request of Mr. Scott to Mr. Lombaert, Carnegie had to take care of an accident that had occurred. To resolve the matter, Carnegie held a court-martial. He relieved the one most responsible for the accident, and two more were also suspended. When Mr. Scott returned, several of the workers that Carnegie had dismissed asked for the case to be reopened, but Mr. Scott refused.

Carnegie actually suspected that Mr. Scott thought Carnegie's actions were too severe, and Carnegie felt this way too. After years of experience, he concluded that severe punishments are always the least effective. Minor punishment was all that was necessary, but forgiveness is best.

This is how he conducted his business. It is sort of a Zen way of doing things, but it worked well for Carnegie in his career.

Years after this incident, when Carnegie became the division superintendent, he felt pity for those who were suspended, and they also had a place in his heart.

Mr. McMillan was a strong Calvinist of the old generation, while his wife was a Calvinist of the new generation. Carnegie and his friends enjoyed being at her events and attended her church. There, Tom Miller, one of Carnegie's friends, had listened to a sermon on predestination. He certainly did not really agree with it, for he later remarked to Mr. McMillan, "Mr. McMillan, if your idea were correct, then your God would be a perfect devil." After having uttered those words, he left, leaving Mr. McMillan completely surprised.

Things were already looking up for Carnegie. His hard work, diligence, and eye on the ball had started to pay off. Mr. Scott walked in one day and asked if Carnegie had $500. He only had $5 but said he could raise it.

Mr. Scott told him that he could buy shares of the Adams Express Company. Carnegie told his mother about it that evening, and she consented to put together the necessary money. She left by train for East Liverpool the next morning, where her brother held investments from farmers. She arrived in in the evening and got the necessary funds. They also mortgaged the Carnegie house. She then returned with the money, and Carnegie gave it to Mr. Scott. With the money fully paid, for the first time in his life, Carnegie owned some of a company's shares—ten shares of the Adams Express Company. what age?

As time went by, Carnegie kept up his usual routine. He came into the office one morning and found a letter addressed to "Andrew Carnegie, Esquire." *Esquire* was a title that Carnegie and the other boys at the railroad company liked. Inside the letter was a check for $10 drawn on the Gold Exchange Bank of New York. There was also the signature of J.C. Babcock, a cashier.

This $10 was the dividend he earned from the Adam Express Company after he bought their shares. It was the first return on an investment that Carnegie made.

Carnegie later showed the check to his friends. They were utterly surprised, and from then on

59

they all decided to accumulate their money and look for opportunities to invest their capital, which they did through small investments here and there and shared it with each other.

Carnegie was rather shy about going into other people's houses. Whenever he delivered a telegram to Mr. Franciscus, the freight agent, Mrs. Franciscus always tried to make him come in, but he never did, and it was years later before she succeeded in making him join in a meal in her house. When Mr. Scott took Carnegie out for a meal at a hotel, however, he was more than happy to attend.

On the one hand, you could consider Carnegie's shyness to be a side of his personality, but he was not really shy. He just appreciated and respected decorum. As an agent of the telegraph company, he was there on a job, and it would be inappropriate to accept an invitation to tea.

When he finally entered Mr. Franciscus' home, he decided that he had never seen a home so wonderful except for the home of another superior, a Mr. Stokes, who had invited Carnegie to his home, although Carnegie could not imagine why. He believed that he had nothing to interest such a learned and intelligent man, who was then the chief counselor of the Pennsylvania Railroad Company. What Andrew liked best about Mr. Stokes' home was a carving on the marble mantel of a bookcase with the words,

"He that cannot reason is a fool,

He that will not a bigot,

He that dare not a slave."

[handwritten annotations:]
- *think for himself — theological*
- *justification forbelief*
- *think rationally*
- *person that is obstinately intolerably devoted to his/her opinions/prejudices*
- *Mr Stokes ?*
- *Following anything blindly w/o questions as to why, etc.*

Carnegie then said to himself that he would someday have a library where he would have a mantel with these words on it, and his plans did come to fruition, for both in Skibo and New York are libraries with these same words.

[handwritten:]
*Skibo Castle
Dornoch, UK*

61

Chapter 5 Life in Altoona

Until this point of his life at the railroad, Mr. Scott was responsible for promoting Carnegie, but both were soon promoted to a higher position at the same time by a higher authority.

Mr. Scott became superintendent of the Pennsylvania Railroad Company in 1856 and took Carnegie with him to Altoona. The move from Pittsburgh to Altoona was not too easy for the Carnegie family, but they were willing to do it, and Carnegie was not going to allow anything to stand in the way of his success.

When Carnegie and Mr. Scott were in Altoona, they first stayed in the railway hotel. Later, however, they would live in a house where Mr. Scott's children would stay. Before Mr. Scott's move to Altoona, his wife had passed away. He now always wanted Carnegie close to him, and he was really the only friend he had in Altoona. The railwaymen in Altoona organized a strike as soon as Mr. Scott took office as superintendent. The men running the trains had stopped their work, causing traffic to pile up. Carnegie was awakened in the middle of the night and informed of the problem. He did not want to wake Mr. Scott because he felt very stressed and was always very nervous. Mr. Scott, however, stirred when Carnegie asked him if he should tend to the problem. Mr. Scott barely managed to give his approval, for he really was only half-awake. Carnegie then slipped out and told the railway men that they could have a hearing the following day at Altoona. The men then continued their work, the trains went on, and the traffic cleared away.

It wasn't just the railwaymen who were ganging up to strike against Mr. Scott, but the shopkeepers were also coming together to strike. Carnegie learned about this while he was walking home one night. A man was following him and soon came up to him and said that Carnegie had once done him a favor, and that he had promised himself to pay it back if he could. The man had earlier called the Pennsylvania Railroad Company in Pittsburgh inquiring about a job as a blacksmith. Carnegie had said that there wasn't any job available in Pittsburgh, but that there might be one in Altoona. Carnegie then asked the man to wait a little while and said that he would check. He checked by telegraph and told the man that the job was available.

The man told Carnegie that he was doing very well, and his family was with him in Altoona as well. He went on to tell Carnegie about the strike. He said that he had learned that several men were signing a paper pledging themselves to strike the next day. Carnegie immediately informed Mr. Scott of the problem, and he at once put up posters in the shop saying that all who had signed the paper were dismissed and were to head to the office to be paid. A list of the names of the people who had signed the paper was received by Mr. Scott and Carnegie, and the fact that they had received the list was announced. Fear and anxiety spread among the workers, and the strike was called off.

Through experience, Carnegie had found that doing favors for people who are disinterested and receiving no reward is better than carrying out a favor and then being repaid for it. It is better to carry out favors for a man who would not be able to repay his "debt" than to do a favor for someone who is capable of returning the favor. The reward for carrying out these favors is simply happiness, which is more important than money or any other sort of payment.

A suit was once brought against the Pennsylvania Railroad Company, and the case was about to be tried by a Major Stokes, who feared that Carnegie might be compelled to attend court by way of a subpoena. He then asked Mr. Scott to send Carnegie out of the state as soon as possible, and Carnegie liked being sent away.

After he had left, he had a rather interesting train ride. He was seated at the back of the carriage in a window seat looking out when a "farmer-looking" man, as he described him, approached him. The man was carrying a small green bag. He said that he had spoken to the brakeman, and the brakeman had told him that Carnegie was with the Pennsylvania Railroad Company. He then said that he wished to show Carnegie an invention. He then pulled out a model of the back of a sleeping car from his small green bag. The sleeping car represented the train carriages meant for night travel. This man was Theodore Tuttle Woodruff, inventor of the sleeping car, a coffee-hulling machine, a steam plow, and a surveyor's compass.

Carnegie was very interested in this invention. He badly wanted to go back and tell Mr. Scott what had happened. When he finally managed to do so, Mr. Scott did not think much of it but was willing to consider it. He told Carnegie that he might call Mr. Woodruff to the office.

After the meeting, they decided that they would try the sleeping cars, and an agreement was made. All that remained was for Mr. Woodruff to begin building the sleepers.

To manufacture them, Mr. Woodruff asked Carnegie for assistance. He needed to get together enough money to pay for the carriage to be built, and he was offering a one-eighth share in the endeavor. He already had the rest of the money he needed to help him build the cars.

The total investment required was to be paid in monthly installments, and Carnegie's share of the payment was one-eighth of the total monthly sum, which amounted to $217.50. Carnegie did not know how he would amass that sort of money on a monthly basis but said that he would do so anyway.

He applied for a loan from a Mr. Lloyd, a banker. Carnegie told him why he needed the loan, and the banker willingly agreed. He told Carnegie, "Why of course I will lend it. You are all right, Andy."

There are two parts of this anecdote that require explanation. The first is that Carnegie had a particular way about him that put those around him at ease, but he was also very conscious of his ⟶

personal trustworthiness. If he said it, he would do it. It is a quality that too many people do not have today. True titans of industry, from Vanderbilt to Ford, could always be relied on to do what they said, and because of that they were always trusted. That may not seem like much, but when the time comes and opportunity presents itself, the need for others to trust you even if they do not like you is important. Carnegie conducted himself with pride and dignity that caused his reputation to precede him. Not only was he capable and willing to take risks, but he was also trusted by his peers and superiors alike to do what he said he would do.

Once he received the loan, he invested the money that was required to build the sleeping cars. In the end, the sleeping cars were a great success, and Carnegie's investment paid off abundantly. He paid off the bank and saved the profits.

The move to Altoona presented as many opportunities as it did challenges, and Carnegie had fared well in navigating almost all of them, but they were not limited to just professional or work-related issues. His life was changing, and his lifestyle was certainly on the upswing, which was something that he was not yet used to.

One time that this was most apparent was when the family was going to hire a servant for the first time. In the past, they had always been alone, living together with no outsider in their home. Carnegie's mother had always been the one to cook and clean the house as well as wash and mend the clothes for her two sons. She was not ready to allow anyone else to handle that. She was their mother, and no one could do what she did. Carnegie, however, managed to convince her to let a servant take care of all the chores. He wanted his mother to rest and take on hobbies and activities to pass her time. After hiring a maid, however, the family was not happy with a servant in the household. Although sufficient and edible, the food served was not as good as that prepared by their mother.

Someone who is surrounded by his or her family and nurtured and raised only by the family is much more privileged and better off than the rich child who is raised in the arms of a governess or some caretaker.

After a servant was hired to take care of the household chores, Carnegie's mother had for the first time the opportunity to go out with her sons, visit her neighbors, and have some fun. She was always of high class and never, according to Carnegie, met anyone who was of equal class.

After Mr. Scott had moved to a house and his children were there as well, he sometimes went off to Philadelphia or other places. While Carnegie stayed in the house of Mr. Scott, his niece, Rebecca Stewart, made things a little more homelike for Carnegie. She was like an older sister to him, and the two became good friends. They went for drives together in the woods in the afternoons, and their friendship endured. Later, they did part, for Rebecca's daughter married the Earl of Sussex, and she was thus always abroad. One time, however, Carnegie and his wife did meet Rebecca, who was at the time already an old woman in widowhood. Carnegie has said that friendships formed in youth can never be replaced.

Mr. Scott and Carnegie stayed in Altoona for about three years. In 1859, Mr. Scott was promoted to vice president of the Pennsylvania Railroad Company, taking Mr. Lombaert's place. Carnegie was deeply affected, as he did not want to be separated from Mr. Scott much less serve another person who would hold his former position. Carnegie also understood that his job in the railway company depended very much on Mr. Scott. So what would happen to him?

After Mr. Scott returned from his interview in Philadelphia, he called Carnegie into his private room. It was then that he confirmed to Carnegie that he had been promoted to the position of vice president.

That was bad enough, but then he was told that a Mr. Enoch Lewis would take Mr. Scott's position, which would mean that Carnegie would be out of a job because the superintendent would hire his own assistant the way Mr. Scott had hired Carnegie.

But Mr. Scott asked Carnegie, "Now about yourself, do you think you could manage the Pittsburgh Division?"

At the time, Carnegie felt that he could do anything, but never before had anyone thought that someone the age of twenty-four could handle the job, and Mr. Scott seemed the last person to want Carnegie as superintendent of the Pittsburgh Division. Carnegie replied that he thought he could. Mr. Scott then went on to tell Carnegie that a Mr. Potts, who was then superintendent of the Pittsburgh Division, was being sent to the transportation department, and Carnegie would take his place. He then went on to discuss Carnegie's salary. He asked, "What salary do you think you should have?" Carnegie was rather offended by Mr. Scott's question.

"Salary?" "What do I care for salary?" He did not care about the money and said that working in the former position of Mr. Scott was good enough for him. He said that the position was more important than the money. He said that he could be paid what he was getting then, which was just $65 a month.

Mr. Scott went on to say that Mr. Potts was being paid $1,800, and he was paid $1,500 when he held the post. He said that Carnegie could start off with $1,500 for his trial, and his salary could be raised to $1,800 if he did well. Carnegie's first job as bobbin boy paid him $5 a month or about $60 a year.

Carnegie then took the job of division superintendent of the Pittsburgh Division, his new position becoming official on December 1, 1859. The Carnegie family then left their home in Altoona and returned to Pittsburgh. The family enjoyed the move, as it meant picking up contacts with old friends. Back in Pittsburgh, Carnegie's younger brother, Tom, would become his secretary, for he had learned telegraphy during his time in Altoona.

The family rented a house on Eighth Street, which then was called Hancock Street.
The city was so dirty with soot in the air that one's hands would be soiled just by touching the balustrade as one ascended the stairs. If you washed your hands and face, they were dirty within an hour. Furthermore, the soot in the air soaked your hair. It really was a rather miserable time for the Carnegie family after having moved from the clean air of the mountains and the refreshing smells of Altoona.

The first winter during Carnegie's time as division superintendent was rather bad. The tracks were not laid properly, being placed on stone and being held by cast-iron chairs. Carnegie said that sometimes as many as forty-seven of these chairs would break in one night. Being division superintendent meant that by night he sent out orders by telegram, and he was always seeing to some wreck or obstruction. The winter, being a bad time for the trains, caused Carnegie to always see some sort of wreck.

He later considered himself to have been the most unmindful of superintendents concerning the condition of the workers. He did not understand what the limits of the human body were and was not accustomed to fatigue, always running on responsibility as his fuel. He could always sleep, and he usually slept thirty minutes or so in a dirty freight car. That was sufficient for him, and he thought everyone was the same way. They weren't.

It was all in all a tough time. Work was hard, the atmosphere was harsh, and the Carnegies had had better. A freight agent that Carnegie knew, a Mr. D.A. Stewart, told Carnegie about a house in Homewood, the neighborhood where he lived.

The Carnegies immediately moved in. Homewood was a place where the rich lived. The residents there were of a higher class, and the surrounding area was clean, smelled better, and was overall more pleasant. Carnegie's mother had the happiest time of her life here, tending to a large garden of several acres. She developed somewhat of a green thumb, and when Carnegie once pulled a weed from the ground, she scolded him, saying that it was something green.

The residents of Homewood usually hosted parties with music, and Carnegie was always invited to these and enjoyed them. The most important family Carnegie met in Homewood was the Wilkins. They were the leading family of Western Pennsylvania, and the most important member of the family was Judge Wilkins. He was eighty years old but still in tip-top mental condition—sharp as a tack. He was rather like history in the flesh for Carnegie. To young Andy, it seemed as if Wilkins really had experienced everything. He always talked about how President Andrew Jackson had said something to him or how he told the Duke of Wellington something. In fact, Wilkins had actually worked as the minister of Andrew Jackson to Russia, and he recounted his interview with the czar.

As Carnegie always attended the classy house parties of the wealthy residents of Homewood, he always heard of things he did not know, and he made it a rule that he would learn something about them immediately. He was rather pleased with himself to find that he was always learning something new every day.

There was only one thing that the Wilkins family and Carnegie did not agree on, and that was politics. Carnegie was an ardent supporter of equality, and the Wilkins family was rather supportive of the South regarding slavery. One day Carnegie entered the home and saw that the household was talking about something very passionately. Mrs. Wilkins then said to him, "What do you think? Dallas writes me that he has been compelled by the commandment of West Point to sit next to a negro! Did you ever hear the like of that? Is it not disgraceful? Negroes admitted to West Point!" Dallas was the lady's grandson. Carnegie then replied, "Oh! Mrs. Wilkins, there is something even worse than that. I understand that some of them have been admitted to heaven!"

What always stood out about Carnegie's personality is that he was direct and vocal but also quite witty.
This trait seems to have come from his mother, who was charming and witty when she needed to be and fiercely protective of her family and the high moral ground. It was never about money but about what was right.

As for the whole Dallas-West Point affair, the entire family said nothing in response to Carnegie's snide retort. Their silence reverberated throughout the house with a din of disapproval. After a short moment, Mrs. Wilkins responded, "That is a different matter, Mr. Carnegie."

Carnegie was very opposed to slavery and a strong supporter of equality. His statement was basically stating that God treated blacks equally, so why were they upset about a black man at West Point?

Soon afterward, Mrs. Wilkins began knitting an afghan for Carnegie. While she was doing this work, people kept asking who it was for, but she didn't tell. Finally, however, when it was complete, it was nearing the time of Christmas, and she wrapped it up as a gift and told her daughter to send it to Carnegie. He received it in New York and kept it as a most precious and valuable possession. He showed it only to a few close friends, but other than that it was not useful for him.

While Carnegie was in Pittsburgh, he met Leila Addison, the daughter of a Dr. Addison. Carnegie considered Leila to be a close friend, for she took the trouble to polish him up. She improved him by teaching and critiquing him. He began to pay more attention to his English and the English classics and read them with great passion.

She also taught Carnegie how to be a little more refined. He found that it was better to speak nicer and on the whole to be well-behaved. Until Carnegie met Leila, he did not care much for his attire, wearing shirts with loose collars and big boots. His entire appearance regarding his clothes was considered strange, although among his associates it was considered manly. Whenever there was anything seen as dapper delicate regarding dressing, Carnegie and his associates looked down on it. One instance of this was when a man of the railway, a gentleman, wore kid gloves. He became the subject of scorn among Carnegie and his associates, for they were the kind of people who wanted to be manly. Thanks to Leila Addison, Carnegie became much more refined and better clothed.

Several years later, after Carnegie became superintendent of the Pennsylvania Railroad Company in Pittsburgh, he once again visited the home of Mr. Stokes, who was a prominent figure in the Democratic Party and talked about how the North was using force to hold the Union together. He did not agree with that. Carnegie then blurted out, "Mr. Stokes, we shall be hanging men like you in less than six weeks." Mr. Stokes laughed at Carnegie's statement and called to his wife, "Nancy, listen to this young Scotch devil. He says they'll be hanging men like me in less than six weeks."

Later, when Carnegie was working in the office of the Secretary of War, Mr. Stokes came to Carnegie trying to be ranked as a major as a volunteer. Thus, Mr. Stokes became Major Stokes.

The man who had earlier criticized the North for how it kept the country united was now fighting for the North. All people cared about at the time of the Civil War was the Union—the unification of the United States. Major Ingersoll once said, "There was not enough air on the American continent to float two." The American people wanted only one American flag. They wanted unity.

Chapter 6 The Civil War

The Civil War began April 12, 1861, and ended May 10, 1865. It was a four-year war that was fought between the Confederacy of the South and the Union forces, commonly known as the North.

The rationale for the war is complicated and not really appropriate to discuss here, but what is important to understand, though, is that the war was one of the defining moments in American history—not just in terms of the moral compass that derived from it but also because it was the defining moment that altered the country from a state-centered power that was fragmented to a federal structure that was stronger in the middle. Carnegie referred to it as a centripetal force versus centrifugal force.

Although this man had little formal education, the nuances of the Civil War were not lost on him, as he realized that a nation that was loosely bound together and concentrated the powers of legislation and control within the limbs of the body versus the power of a central and fortified federal system were like the centrifugal force versus the centripetal force, respectively.

Then there was another aspect of the war that made something else clear to him. Coming from an immigrant background, it was easy for him to see that it was important to be one country united against its external challenges than to be divided within the country fighting for transient differences. It was important that disagreements could be decided at the ballot box. Once the ballots were cast, the decision was made. No need for referendums. After the end of the Civil War, the United States turned every ballot cast for every state and federal office into a referendum on what was being proposed. The country chose what their candidate was advocating as the way to voice their choice on the matter. Carnegie could see that clearly.

In essence, this was what was supposed to have happened with the election of Abraham Lincoln. In setting up the election, the platform they stood on served as the platform the population wanted. If one stands for slavery and one stands for emancipation, then the winning candidate shows that the platform he stood on is what the constituents want, but that wasn't the case with the election that Lincoln won. The Democratic Party had split the vote by fielding two candidates, and Lincoln won the majority with only 40% of the vote.

Lincoln may have been right on the moral spectrum of reality, but it was not what the South wanted. To them slavery was a way of life, and the reason for the Civil War was because any changes in the status quo would have brought about significant repercussions to their competitive advantage on world markets. Slaves were not paid, and if they had to hire people to do their work, they had to pay them a salary, thus putting a strain on their profits.

The South had seceded from the North, and Northerners did not respect this new nation. They did not believe in the legitimacy of secession because they feared that the United States might be broken down into several states that saw each other as enemies. Northerners wanted unity.

The beginning of the Civil War started when the Confederate Army opened fire on Fort Sumter in Charleston, South Carolina. They forced the fort to surrender, and the United States flag was taken down. President Lincoln called for the uprising to be put down, and in response, four more slave states severed all ties with the North and joined the Confederacy.

From 1862 to 1865, the Confederate army under the leadership of General Robert E. Lee repelled the attacks of the Union army that was commanded by a string of incapable commanders. Finally, in 1864, General Ulysses S. Grant became commander of the Union armies and after many battles, such as The Wilderness, Cold Harbor, Petersburg, and Spotsylvania, Grant was able to corner Lee at Appomattox in Virginia.

While this was happening, Union armies were able to win several victories over the Southerners in the Southern states west of the Appalachian Mountain range. Between 1864 and 1865, General William Tecumseh Sherman led his Union soldiers into Confederate hubs, such as Georgia and Virginia. By 1865, practically all Confederate armies had surrendered, and finally on May 10, 1865, the president of the Confederacy, Jefferson Davis, was taken prisoner while trying to escape. All resistance from the South was put down, and the bloody four-year war was at an and.

The Civil War resulted in the deaths of 625,000 American soldiers, which was nearly the same number of U.S. soldiers killed in all the wars the nation had ever fought, combined. The Civil War was the most devastating conflict of the West after the Napoleonic Wars from 1803 to 1815 and the First World War.

Carnegie was very much opposed to slavery and to all war. He was a strong advocate of freedom for all and condemned slavery and racism. We have seen that when he heard his friends, the Wilkins, talking about how it was a disgrace that one of their relatives had to sit next to a Negro, he replied by saying that God treated them equally, and yet they were making a fuss. Carnegie repeatedly made his point about the sense of equality that was important in the building of a young nation. It was also the morally right thing to do.

At the start of the Civil War in 1861, Carnegie received a telegram from his old boss Mr. Scott. He was told to come to Washington, D.C. posthaste. Carnegie was unaware that Mr. Scott had been appointed Assistant Secretary of War in charge of the Department of Transportation. The Secretary of War at that time was Simon Cameron.

To be clear, there was no Department of Defense during the Lincoln Administration. It wasn't until 1947 when that department was created. Until then it was called the War Department.

When Carnegie reached Washington, Mr. Scott told him that his country needed him. Mr. Scott needed an assistant for his new position in the Transportation Department, and he wanted Carnegie to fill that post.

As Mr. Scott's assistant, Carnegie was to be in charge of the railways and government telegrams.

Carnegie was exhilarated. He had not expected to have such a position in government, but he gladly accepted the job and left Pittsburgh.

His first duty was to put together a force of railwaymen and head to Baltimore. Some Union troops that were passing through Baltimore had been attacked, and the railway line that stretched from Baltimore to Annapolis Junction had been severed. This cut off all communication with Washington.

Carnegie's duty was to take his group of assistants to the site and repair the damage. When they arrived, they began to repair the tracks so that heavy trains could use it safely.

This job lasted a few days. By the time General Butler and his troops arrived, Carnegie had repaired the tracks, and the general and his men were able to go on to Washington.

On their way to Washington, Carnegie realized that some of the telegraph lines had been staked. He called for the train to come to a stop and then ran down to free the lines. He did not notice, however, that the lines had been pushed to one side before staking, and when he released the wires, they sprang up and struck him in the cheek, causing his face to bleed heavily.

Carnegie said that except for a few other soldiers who were wounded in Baltimore he was among the first to shed blood for his country. He was willing to do anything for the country that had done so much for him, and he worked night and day to try and establish communications with the South.

Shortly afterward, Carnegie established his headquarters in Alexandria, Virginia, and while there the Battle of Bull Run was fought, a battle in which Confederate troops defeated Union soldiers. Carnegie then sent out trains to pick up the retreating soldiers. The closest station was Burke Station, and Carnegie traveled there and began loading trains with wounded soldiers. It became clear that the station had to be closed, and the operator and Carnegie were the last to leave.

Everyone was in a state of panic. Some conductors and engineers were able to obtain boats and cross the Potomac. Some of the railwaymen were missing. All in all, most of the railwaymen did not flee nor did any of the telegraphers.

After this experience, Carnegie established his headquarters in Washington once more with Mr. Scott, who was now Colonel Scott. Being in charge of the telegraph allowed Carnegie to meet President Abraham Lincoln, Secretary Cameron, Mr. Seward, and other important people. Lincoln would usually come to his desk either waiting for a reply to a telegram or just seeking further information.

Carnegie's perspective of Lincoln indicates that he was a homely man when he was relaxed. He has described Lincoln as having so many features that it was impossible to portray him properly in a painting. When he was animated or telling story, he would be bright and energetic. Lincoln was always attentive to what everyone had to say. Carnegie has also mentioned that Lincoln had a unique way of talking.

On November 8, 1861, Confederate diplomats James Slidell and John Murray Mason were taken prisoner by Charles Wilkes, captain of the Union ship the *USS San Jacinto* while they were aboard the British mail ship, the *HMS Trent*.
Prior to this, on May 13, 1861, Queen Victoria of Great Britain made Britain neutral regarding the American Civil War, although the British press supported the Confederacy, and many British citizens secretly funded the Confederates.

The British were very serious about not letting anyone step onto their ship without permission much less capturing people on their ships. Thus, the arrest of Mr. Slidell and Mr. Mason was going to result in either war between the Union and Britain, or the Americans would have to return the Confederates.

Lincoln's Cabinet convened to discuss the matter. At the time, Secretary Cameron was not able to attend, and Mr. Scott was to take his place at the meeting as Assistant Secretary of War. Before the meeting, Carnegie tried to convince Mr. Scott to argue to return the prisoners, for, as he said, the British would wage war because of what had happened. Furthermore, it was American policy that ships were not to be searched. Mr. Scott, however, was inclined to keep the prisoners, but after the meeting, he told Carnegie that Seward had said that it meant war, concurring with what Carnegie had said. Lincoln was also more inclined to keep the prisoners but soon agreed to Seward's plan. It was decided, however, that no action was to be taken until those who were absent, including Secretary Cameron, could be consulted on the matter. Thus, Mr. Scott was instructed to discuss the matter with Cameron the next day when he arrived, for it was believed that he was in no mood to relinquish the prisoners.

In the beginning, those who were in charge of handling problems were rather incapable of doing so. They were old, handicapped men, such as General Scott. The question was how to manage situations when these old men were taking days to come up with an answer to a problem that needed quick action. How were they to rely on leaders that did not fully understand what was happening?

Soon, however, much to Carnegie's surprise, matters began to work well. Secretary Cameron gave Colonel Scott the authority to do things as he saw fit. This was a very good position to be in, for Carnegie and Mr. Scott could now do what they saw was best. Soon, Secretary Cameron was dismissed by Lincoln, for the public was calling for his dismissal. Those who worked with Lincoln, however, knew that if the other departments had been run as well as the War Department under Cameron things would have gone a lot better.

Cameron, who liked to be called Lochiel, when ninety years old, visited Carnegie in Scotland, where the two men rode through the glens, and Cameron told Carnegie how he had secured second terms for two U.S. presidents, James K. Polk and Abraham Lincoln. He had drawn up new resolutions for a certain state and hoped that other states would follow. He used this strategy to secure a second term for both Polk and Lincoln. One day Cameron went to Lincoln's public reception in Washington. Lincoln called out to him and said, "Two more today, Cameron, two more." That meant that two more states had passed the Jackson-Lincoln Resolutions.

What's important here is how one man was called by two presidents from different times to seek advice about the same thing.

The next person that should be mentioned is General Ulysses S. Grant, who was also the eighteenth president of the United States. Grant appeared to be an remarkable man. He had the looks of someone who was a nobody, yet he was very accomplished. Once, when the Secretary of War, Stanton, had Grant and three of his associates enter his car, he looked at them, and once they were all inside, he thought that one of them was Grant, but *this* one wasn't. *This* one *was* Grant.

Carnegie himself was sometimes mistaken as Ulysses S. Grant.

Carnegie found that when Grant was general there was a lot of talk about strategy and how to do things. Grant was very open with Carnegie about these things and did not keep anything hidden. Once he said that he was instructed to go east and said that he would. He said that he was just going to go west to get everything ready. Carnegie replied by saying, "I thought as much." Grant went on to say that he was going to put Sherman in charge. Carnegie responded by saying that it was expected that General Thomas would be the one to succeed. Grant responded by saying he knew this but said the men and Thomas both thought that Sherman should be chosen. He went on to say that they were winning in the West and now had to win in the East.

Once when Grant was in the West, he started to drink a little too much. Finally, after some time, his chief of staff, Rawlins, mentioned his drinking problem. At first, Grant said, "You do not mean that? I was wholly unconscious of it. I am surprised!" Rawlins responded by saying, "Yes, I do mean it. It is even beginning to be a subject of comment among your officers." Grant replied by saying, "Why did you not tell me before? I'll never drink a drop of liquor again."

Grant did not say this in passing. He really did mean it, and he kept his word for as long as he lived. When Carnegie dined with the Grants, he noticed that Grant always turned down wine. He never drank after Rawlins told him that his drinking was a problem. Grant's willingness and strength of mind was what prevented him from breaking his word. Not many people can abstain from alcohol for life. One of Carnegie's associates once abstained from alcohol for three years but then relapsed into drinking again.

When Grant became president, charges were raised that he was accepting money dishonestly. Those who were wiser, however, understood that he was really so poor that he had to cancel his attendance at traditional state dinners, which cost him $800 each time. When his annual salary as president was raised from $25,000 to $50,000, he was able to save a little money, but he did not care for it.

When Grant was at the end of his first term, Carnegie understood that he had virtually no money, yet when he was in Europe, he found that high officials there believed Grant had benefited. In America, people knew how to brush away these accusations, but in other countries they seemed quite real.

The reason democracy does not do too well in such places as Britain is because American politics is thought to be corrupt, and that Republicanism is the main cause of this corruption. Carnegie thought that in such countries as Britain bribery was common in land holdings, but such matters were considered titles rather than bribes.

When Carnegie was summoned to Washington in 1861, people thought that the Civil War would end very quickly, but soon it became clear that it would be a matter of years. After some time, Mr. Scott realized that Carnegie was needed in Pittsburgh to manage the Pittsburgh Division of the Pennsylvania Railroad Company. The railroad company badly needed Carnegie's attention, for the American government was placing a major strain on it during this time. Mr. Scott and Carnegie then left Washington and returned to their former duties, Mr. Scott carrying on his work as vice president of the Pennsylvania Railroad Company and Carnegie as superintendent of the Pittsburgh Division.

After leaving Washington, Carnegie suffered his first important illness. He experienced what felt like sunstroke. After consulting with his physician, he was told that he could no longer be in the heat, and the summers of America were not suitable for him. Carnegie felt that the air in the Highlands, being clean and cool, would be a universal cure for him.

Later, his leave was approved by the Pennsylvania Railroad Company, and he, his mother, and his friend Tom Miller returned to Scotland, their homeland. They boarded the steamer *Etna* and landed in Liverpool. From there, they headed straight for Dunfermline. As they approached, Carnegie's mother caught sight of a familiar bush and cried out, "Oh! There's the broom! There's the broom!" Carnegie tried to calm her, but in doing so she only felt happier.

Carnegie himself felt that he might be able to kiss the ground.

When they arrived in Dunfermline, Carnegie was quite surprised by how small everything seemed. He felt as if he were walking in a city of the Lilliputians, the tiny people mentioned in Jonathan Swift's *Gulliver's Travels*. He described it as if he could almost touch the roofs that extended over the sides of the houses, and that walking the full length of the beach now felt very short, for it was really only three miles. Furthermore, he felt that the grounds on which he had played as a boy were now very small, and that the houses he previously felt to be grand and magnificent were also very small. In short, everything had shrunk for him.

The feeling must have been very peculiar, but the explanation is perhaps quite simple. He had left Dunfermline and Scotland when he was just a boy, and this was the first time that he was returning to Scotland in more than a decade. When he left, everything towered over him. Now he was twenty-seven years old and felt the size of Dunfermline to be like what any other adult of Dunfermline felt it to be, only it seemed rather small, for his last memories of his hometown were when he was a young lad.

Everything seemed to have shrunk for Carnegie, but what still appeared to be as grand was the abbey. Still on the tower were the words "King Robert the Bruce," whom he had learned so much about as a young boy with his cousin, Dod, from his Uncle Lauder. Everything, even the well at the head of Moodie Street from which he had collected water and argued with old ladies, seemed different.

To Carnegie, though, Dunfermline Abbey was still magnificent, and its bell still rang sweetly in his ear. The area around the abbey seemed small, but all soon came back to normal in his mind after hearing the abbey bell and seeing the magnificent site.

Carnegie's relatives were very kind to him and his mother, the kindest of all being his Aunt Charlotte, who said, "Oh, you will just be coming back here some day and keep a shop in the High Street." To her, to have a shop in the High Street was a success.

Carnegie's Aunt Charlotte had sometimes taken care of Carnegie when he was young and told him stories that he had to be fed with two spoons, for he screamed whenever the spoon left his mouth. Later, when Carnegie was in the steel business, Captain Jones said that he had been "born with two rows of teeth with holes punched for more." Carnegie really was always pushing for better results.

Other stories he was told included one where his father had to carry him back for some distance from the sea. While walking up the steep hills, his father hinted about the heavy load on his back, hoping that Carnegie might offer to walk for a little while. To his surprise, however, Carnegie responded by saying, "Ah, father, never mind. Patience and perseverance make the man, ye ken."

His father laughed and continued to walk up the hill with Andrew on his back. Carnegie felt best when he was once again with his Uncle Lauder, who had taught him so much and had made him like literature when he was just eight years old. Carnegie was called "Naig" by his uncle just as he had been when he was a young lad.

During Carnegie's stay in Dunfermline, he was so excited that he just could not sleep. He soon caught a cold and tried to recover by spending six weeks in his uncle's house. Soon, however, he was not getting any better and was forced to return to the United States. During the journey, he began to recover and felt so good that he could return to his work duties at once.

On his way back to his office, the railwaymen of the Pennsylvania Railroad Company under Carnegie welcomed him warmly, and Carnegie was glad to see that the caring feelings he had for them were returned. According to him, working men always reciprocate kindness.

Chapter 7 Trains, Tracks, and Opportunity

Once locomotives were introduced to the New World, they went through a period of rapid growth and then some slow periods, as the fragmented industry went through consolidation. Cornelius Vanderbilt had maneuvered the landscape and set the industry on its trajectory with a series of consolidations that made the services more organized and efficient.

Then it was time for growth again, but this time there was a need for a different sort of infrastructure to fuel the growth. America was, and still is, a land of hills, plains, and rivers, and building around them was expensive. It was better to use bridges to conquer ravines, but the technology was not there to develop the proper designs. Bridges had already been built, but many had collapsed, and constant maintenance was often needed. The culprit, it turned out, was the material. Even iron easily eroded under the stress and strain of the repeated passing locomotive. In time, bridges weakened and failed.

Then there was another problem. Aside from the bridges that carried the rails, the rails themselves were not hardy. In the mid-19th century, a passenger in one of the open cars could see slivers of shiny iron particles in the air that come off the rails. Each wheel that rolled on the rail would take off a bit of metal, and the rail would later become deformed and warped and come off.

The weakness of the material was a key issue, and Carnegie was one of the men who figured this out early in the game when he had to keep attending to breakdowns and crashes.

Aside from high replacement, rail lines were being extended. More lines covering more cities and over greater distances were needed across the rapidly growing country. The second half of the 1800s was America's greatest period of growth, and railroads were the driving factor behind it.

Carnegie took advantage of the situation and put together a company that built railway lines, but instead of building them with iron, he adopted the system that was created in Britain by Sir Henry Bessemer.

With his friend Thomas N. Miller, Andrew Carnegie also established a company called Pittsburgh Locomotive Works, which built trains. This company rapidly became popular and was a formidable competitor to other companies that had been in existence for much longer.

It all started when Carnegie saw a bridge in Altoona that had been built by the Pennsylvania Railroad Company with iron rather than wood. It worked flawlessly. He understood that it was the iron that made it work so well.

This was in contrast to other wooden or iron bridges belonging to the Pennsylvania Railroad

Company that had burned and caused massive delays in traffic for up to eight days. Seeing the opportunity this presented, Carnegie called a meeting with three men: Mr. H.J. Linville, Mr. Schiffler, and John L. Piper. Piper and Schiffler were in charge of the bridges for Pennsylvania Railroad, while Mr. Linville was responsible for the bridge design. Carnegie invited the three men to put together a company that built bridges, but this time they were going to make cast-iron bridges that could withstand the heat of a fire and the weight of the locomotive. Carnegie was also able to convince Mr. Scott to join the project.

A company that built bridges, as Carnegie proposed to make, had never existed before and had great investment potential. When Carnegie invested in Mr. Woodruff's sleeping-coach company, he reaped substantial profits. Just by investing $217.50, he made more than $5,000 per year on it for many years after.

Carnegie also grew more acute with investing as he grew older. In this case, he saw a specific opportunity in bridges and the way they were constructed.

Scott, Linville, Piper, Schiffler, and Carnegie each paid one-fifth interest of $1,250. Carnegie borrowed the money for his share from the bank.

The Keystone Bridge Works came about in 1862. Carnegie felt intense pride in the name he gave the company, seeing that Pennsylvania was the Keystone State.

At this time, iron bridges were rather popular in the United States, but for Carnegie's company it was cast-iron. Some of the bridges that had been built were later modified to support heavier traffic.

Shortly after the company was established, it was commissioned to build a bridge across the Ohio River. Steel was not yet popular and wrought-iron had only just come into use. When the president of the Erie Railroad Company came to inspect the progress, he said to

Carnegie, "I don't believe these heavy castings can be made to stand up and carry themselves much less carry a train across the Ohio River."

After the bridge was built, it was modified to handle heavier traffic and was in service for some time. The profit Carnegie and his company would have made from building the bridge would have been impressive except for inflation. To compensate for the loss of present value, the president of the Pennsylvania Railroad Company, Edgar Thomson, allowed Carnegie and his company to charge more money. He said that before the bridge had been built no one had considered what might be the state of the economy after the job was completed.

Carnegie has described Piper, Schiffler, and Linville as incredible geniuses. President Thomson once remarked that he would rather have Piper at the scene of a burning bridge than the entire engineering corps. As smart as he was, however, Piper had one weakness that was rather beneficial to Carnegie. Piper would often drop whatever he was doing for horses, which turned out to be a chink in his armor.

Seeing that Piper would do anything for horses, Carnegie and others used horses as an excuse to get him to do things. If they wanted him to take a break, they would send him someplace with horses where he could look after them. Carnegie and his associates would also entrust Piper with choosing horses for them. His love of horses, however, also caused him to get into unfavorable circumstances. Carnegie recounts that Piper once showed up at the office with his shirt torn, his hat missing, his face smeared with dirt, and holding a whip. He said one of the reins had snapped when he was riding fast, and the horse lost its direction or he lost his "steerage way" as he called it.

Piper was often known as "Pipe." When he became friends with someone, he was their friend forever and always loyal. In the beginning, this relationship concerned him and Carnegie, and he transferred his loyalty to Carnegie's young brother, Thomas. Carnegie was still a dear friend of Piper's, but Carnegie's brother was much larger in Piper's eyes. Whatever he said, the colonel believed and accepted.

Piper sometimes argued with managers of steel mills about quality and price as well as other matters. He once went to Carnegie's brother to complain that arrangements he had made for the supply of steel for a year was not taken down correctly. He said there was something about "net," and he didn't understand what this meant. Carnegie's brother said to him, "Well, colonel, it means that nothing more is to be added." Piper replied, "All right, Thomas," and he was happy again. Carnegie has noted that it is important how one says something, for if Thomas had said, "Nothing is to be deducted," it would've caused problems.

It was one of those things about the Carnegies that was different from most other titans in nineteenth century America. Not only did Carnegie have an eye for opportunity and did what was necessary to cultivate and profit from it, but he was also able to communicate effectively.

Another incident that proved the point of the art of conversation happened when Piper was once reading Bradstreet's volume about business concerns. He saw that the rating for the Keystone Bridge Company was "BC," meaning Bad Credit. He was so infuriated that it took some effort to hold him back from going to the company's lawyers and suing the publishers! Thomas Carnegie, however, knew how to placate Piper. He said their company was rated Bad Credit because it had never borrowed anything, and the colonel was happy again.

Another notable character of Carnegie's life during his bridge-building days was a Captain Eads from St. Louis. He had drawn up plans for a bridge that spanned from St. Louis, Missouri, to East St. Louis, Illinois. The bridge was named after its designer, James Buchanan Eads. It was called Eads Bridge.

Captain Eads had drawn up the plans and submitted them to the Keystone Bridge Company. Carnegie sent those plans to a Mr. Linville, whom he considered the best expert on bridges in the entire nation. Linville later reported to Carnegie that the plans were flawed, and that the bridge wouldn't be able to hold its weight if built from their original design. Carnegie then told him to meet with Eads and point this out. He told him to help Eads get the bridge into better shape.

Everything went well at first, and construction of the bridge began. Piper, however, was not able to keep up with Eads' demands. He was at first very pleased to have the Keystone Bridge Company been given the largest contract the company had ever received. Thus, in the beginning, Piper was very happy and treated Captain Eads very well. At this time, he greeted him with the cheerful "Colonel Eads, how do you do? Delighted to see you." He didn't call him Captain Eads in the beginning. After some time, though, Piper became less and less friendly with him, and the greeting degraded to "Good morning, Captain Eads." Soon, Piper was heard referring to him as "Mr. Eads." Later, it became simply "Jim Eads."

After the bridge was complete, Carnegie kept Piper with him in St. Louis to guard the bridge, for threats had been made that the bridge would be torn down. Soon, Piper relieved the guards from protecting the bridge and at the same time began to miss home. He wanted to go back to Pittsburgh and was determined to take the night train back home. Nothing could change his mind—except horses.

When Carnegie tried to think about how to convince Piper to stay with him, he finally hit the jackpot, realizing that he could take advantage of his weakness and use horses to make him stay. Thus, during the day, Carnegie spoke to Piper that he wished to get his sister some horses. He said that St. Louis was a good place for them and asked Piper if he had seen anything nice. Piper immediately began to describe them. He decided to help Carnegie and dropped his plans to return to Pittsburgh that night. Piper chose a wonderful pair of horses, but now the issue was transporting them. He did not want them sent by train, and no boat could take them at the time. This problem would keep Piper in St. Louis until those horses were on their way, and it is no exaggeration to say that he might have gone on the ship with the horses.

The Keystone Bridge Company was the most remarkable iron bridge-building company in the nation. All other companies that had built iron bridges had failed. Some of them collapsed, causing some of the most devastating train accidents in the United States. In contrast, no bridge built by the Keystone Bridge Company ever collapsed. Carnegie's company never built a structure that was not safe or not in sync with the modern world. If they were submitted with an unsafe structure, they would at once reject the job. Some of the Keystone bridges even withstood severe winds, while bridges of other companies collapsed. Carnegie has denied that luck was the reason for his company's success.

Rather, it was because they knew what they were doing, and that is why they were successful.

Carnegie observed that the key to success was the way the Keystone Bridge Company was run. When you focus on the quality of your work, you, your business, and everything you do will be successful. According to him, in the beginning, your work will be difficult until you establish your quality. Once that is done, your business can go on easily. For any business, quality is of prime importance. Everything else, even cost, comes second.

Carnegie devoted several years of his life to his bridge-building company. When there were large contracts to be accepted or declined, he would often go himself to meet the customer. Once he traveled to Dubuque, Iowa, in 1868 with the engineer of the Keystone Bridge Works, Walter Katte.

Apparently, a bridge-building company from Chicago was trying to secure the contract. This company had been awarded the contract by the board, but Carnegie did not leave. He stayed and talked with a number of directors, all of whom did not know right from left regarding the benefits of wrought iron over cast iron. They simply didn't understand the danger of using cast iron. The Keystone Bridge Works had always used wrought-iron to build the upper cord of their bridges, and the Chicago bridge-building company used cast iron. Carnegie described what would happen if a steamer were to strike the cast-iron or the wrought-iron cord. In the case of the wrought-iron cord, the cord would simply bend, but no substantial damage would be inflicted. In contrast, if a steamer were to strike a cast-iron cord, the entire bridge would crash down.

Only one of the directors was able to understand Carnegie's explanation, and that man was Perry Smith, who had once had an accident where he crashed his buggy into a cast-iron lamppost, which cracked on impact. Carnegie said that if only a little more money could be paid, they would have a superbly strong bridge that would not collapse if hit by a steamer. Carnegie went on to say that none of his bridges had ever fallen.

Senator Allison, who became a friend of Carnegie's, asked for Carnegie to leave the room for a moment. Shortly afterward, he was called back in and given the contract for the bridge under the condition that they could pay Carnegie's firm the lower price, which was lower by several thousand dollars, and Carnegie agreed. With that, the Keystone Bridge Company was awarded a prestigious contract even if it was a little less profitable.

Furthermore, it also meant the start of a friendship between Senator Allison and Andrew Carnegie.

What you should extract from this anecdote is that if you want a contract awarded to your firm as Carnegie did, always be at present and ready to accept it. Furthermore, always remember that a seemingly unimportant thing, such as the cast-iron lamppost in this case, might just help you get what you want.

Carnegie's advice is that if you want to get the contract, stay in it until you get it. When Carnegie was in Dubuque, he was told that he could go back home, and the contract would be sent to him. Carnegie turned down this offer and stayed until he was given the contract.

After Carnegie's bridge-building company had built the Steubenville bridge, the Baltimore and Ohio Railroad Company, the oldest railroad company in the nation and one of the fiercest competitors of the Pennsylvania Railroad Company, had to build bridges over the Ohio River from Parkersburg to Wheeling. During the time that Carnegie was trying to have his company awarded the contract, he had the pleasure of a meeting a Mr. Garrett, the president of the Baltimore and Ohio Railroad Company.

Carnegie and his associates wanted to be awarded the contract for the Baltimore and Ohio's bridges over the Ohio River. Mr. Garrett, however, was not too inclined to award the contract to Keystone Bridge Works, believing that they would simply not be able to finish the bridges in the allotted time. He wanted to build the bridges himself. He also asked Carnegie whether or not he could use the designs of the Keystone Bridge Works for his bridges. Carnegie willingly gave Mr. Garrett permission to use the patents of his firm, feeling that approval from the Baltimore and Ohio was important.

Mr. Garrett soon became friends with Carnegie and even invited him to his private room, where they chatted. Garrett told Carnegie about his problems and arguments with the president and vice president of the Pennsylvania Railroad Company, Mr. Thomson and Mr. Scott. This prompted Carnegie to say that when he was on his way to meet Mr. Garrett he had met with Mr. Scott, who asked him where he was going. Carnegie told Mr. Scott that he was going to see Mr. Garrett to be awarded the bridge contracts.

Mr. Scott replied by telling Carnegie that he seldom did anything pointless but he was doing so now, for Mr. Garrett would absolutely not award the contract to Carnegie's firm. The reason for this was that Carnegie was once in the service of the Pennsylvania Railroad Company, a major competitor of the Baltimore and Ohio. When Carnegie had finished, Mr. Garrett said that he did not care who used to work for whom but only for the benefits of his company. He did not care if Carnegie once worked for his greatest rival. All he cared about was the good of his company. He was thus quite willing to give Carnegie the contract.

In the beginning, the terms of the Keystone Bridge Works in building the Ohio bridges were not too favorable for Carnegie, for his firm was given all the difficult bits, while Garrett was going to build all the smaller items in his own shops and use the designs of the Keystone Bridge Works. Carnegie's firm was going to build the dangerous parts, while Garrett built the parts that could earn him money. Carnegie later confronted Garrett on the matter, asking him whether or not he was doing it because he wasn't confident that Carnegie's firm could finish the job at the end of the allotted time. Garrett was concerned, but Carnegie responded by telling him that he did not have to fret over the matter.

Carnegie asked Mr. Garrett whether or not a personal bond of his could be accepted as collateral. If the bridges were not finished by the allotted time, Carnegie would pay Mr. Garrett a certain sum. Mr. Garrett agreed, and Carnegie asked how much he wanted if his firm failed to meet the schedule. Mr. Garrett asked for $100,000. Carnegie promptly accepted the challenge, telling him that his company would not allow him to fork out $100,000, and Mr. Garrett replied by saying that Carnegie's company would indeed not stop working until the bridges were complete to save Carnegie that amount of money.

This, in the end, is why the contract was awarded to Keystone Bridge Works. Carnegie's company was able to build the bridges by the time stated, and Carnegie never had to pay even a penny.

Carnegie and those who worked at the Keystone Bridge Works understood what it meant to build a bridge over the Ohio River more than even Mr. Garrett did. It was not an easy task. Carnegie's company began work on the superstructure of the bridge and left it on the banks of the river. He waited for the completion of the substructure, which was then being built in Mr. Garrett's shops.

Soon, the friendship between Mr. Garrett and Carnegie consolidated, and Mr. Garrett brought Carnegie to his mansion in the countryside. It was supposedly magnificent, with a large area of green grass, and the land was dotted with horses, dogs, sheep, and cows.

Eventually, Mr. Garrett decided that the Baltimore and Ohio Railroad Company should begin to build its own railways. He planned to use the Bessemer process, in which the impure materials of the iron were removed by blowing air through the metal when it was still in its molten state. He had already asked for permission to use this process. Carnegie understood that this was far from beneficial for the Baltimore and Ohio, understanding that the company could buy its rails for the same cost it takes to build only a small number. Carnegie thus traveled to meet Mr. Garrett and went over his plans with him.

Mr. Garrett took Carnegie and several other people who worked for him to the quay where imported goods were arriving by steamship. While the goods were being unloaded from the ships and placed into railway cars, he explained to Carnegie why it was necessary for the Baltimore and Ohio to build its own rails. He said, "Mr. Carnegie, you can now begin to appreciate the magnitude of our vast system and understand why it is necessary that we should make everything for ourselves, even our steel rails. We cannot depend upon private concerns to supply us with any of the principal articles we consume. We shall be a world to ourselves."

Garrett basically meant that the Baltimore and Ohio needed so much that buying them from outsiders would not meet the demands of the company. Carnegie understood that Garrett's idea would not work and replied by saying that his system wasn't really a "vast system." Carnegie went on to say that he saw the last annual report of the Baltimore and Ohio and noticed that the company and received $14 million simply by transporting goods of other people. He went on to say that his own companies had made the items themselves and made even more money. He finished by saying, "You are really a very small concern compared with Carnegie Brothers and Company."

As it turned out, the Baltimore and Ohio did not become a competitor of Carnegie Brothers and Company, as Carnegie's firm built steel rails. The friendship between Carnegie and Mr. Garrett continued, and Mr. Garrett once gave Carnegie a dog that he himself had grown. It was a Scotch collie. Mr. Garrett did not mind in the least that Carnegie was in the service of the Pennsylvania Railroad Company, his company's greatest rival. That fact was surpassed by the friendship between the two men.

Chapter 8 Steel & Oil

Carnegie, Thomas N. Miller, a man by the name of Henry Phipps, and Andrew Kloman started a steel mill. Miller was a dear friend of Carnegie and the backbone of the entire venture of Carnegie, Phipps, and Kloman. In his later years, Tom became more relaxed and sedate, and his views on theology much friendlier and welcoming.

Andrew Kloman was a German mechanic who was very skilled in building excellent pieces of machinery or things needed for structures. Everything he made was expensive, but his products always worked well. Carnegie heard about him when he was a division superintendent for the Pennsylvania Railroad. He found out that Mr. Kloman made a fine axle.

Kloman was really the first person to use the cold saw to cut cold iron. He invented a machine that could make bridge links, called upsetting machines. When Captain Eads was building the

St. Louis bridge and could not acquire the right couplings, Kloman stepped up and said that he could make them and explained why the contractors responsible for doing so were not able to follow up.

Carnegie and his partners were deeply confident in the German and gave him the job. He was able to construct the right couplings, and all went well.

At the same time, Carnegie was already a friend of the Phipps family, the elder brother of Henry, John, being Carnegie's closest friend in the family. Henry was many years younger than Carnegie, but he did catch Carnegie's attention as being particularly smart. Henry once asked John to lend him a quarter, and John gave it to him without question. The following morning, an advertisement in the *Pittsburgh Dispatch* read: "A willing boy wishes work."

This was what Henry had done with the quarter. Instead of buying sweets and candy, the young man found employment. Shortly afterward, the company, Dilworth and Bidwell, called Henry and offered him a job. His parents approved, and he became an errand boy. His first job was to sweep the office.

His importance in the company grew, and he worked his way up to eventually being one of the richest men in the United States. Soon, Phipps caught the attention of Thomas Miller and Andrew Kloman, who both invested in him. It wasn't much, but it was something.

This led to the building of an iron mill on Twenty-Ninth Street.

Carnegie's brother, Thomas, had been a close friend of Phipps. They had spent their lives together and worked very closely with each other.

Henry Phipps spent his money on building conservatories and public parks. He once said they were to be open only on Sundays. This caused a tumultuous uproar among the church ministers, who called for his condemnation. The people, however, did not support the church ministers. Instead, they accepted the gift happily. Phipps once told the ministers, "It is all very well for you, gentlemen, who work one day in the week and are masters of your time the other six during which you can view the beauties of Nature—all very well for you—but I think it shameful that you should endeavor to shut out from the toiling masses all that is calculated to entertain and instruct them on the only day which you well know they have at their disposal."

This was a nice way of saying that the church ministers had all the time in the world, and on the one day a week that the people could take a break, the ministers force them to gather in a church to listen to long and boring sermons.

Church ministers also argued about whether or not to have music in their churches, and while they were debating this subject, other people were doing it for the public good. There was and still is a stark contrast between the attitudes and the way ministers spend their time compared with the attendees of the churches. As it turns out, the holy men are the losers.

While Carnegie was in the steel business, Kloman and Phipps pushed Miller out of their business. Carnegie immediately stood up for his friend, and the two of them created Cyclops Mills, which was launched in 1864. After their mill became successful, Carnegie united the mill of Miller and himself with that of Kloman and Phipps, forming the Union Iron Mills in 1867. Unfortunately, Miller did not know how to forgive his two former business partners and was adamant about not joining in the business venture. It was planned that Carnegie, his brother, and Miller would hold the controlling interest. Miller, however, was not going to work with the people who had shunned him. He even asked Carnegie to buy his part of the interest, and Carnegie sadly did so, feeling that there was no changing Miller's mind. Much later, Miller confessed to Carnegie that he was sorry he did not take Carnegie up on his offer, for if he had he would have shared in the millions of dollars that the business provided.

In the steel mills under Carnegie and his partners, the products were of excellent quality. Nothing was ever faulty. The firm was very productive and often built what other firms were not building but whose demand was increasing. A strict rule in Carnegie's steel business was that he would build whatever other steel businesses would not.

As time went by, Carnegie found that no steel manufacturer ever knew how much money he had made or lost until they closed the books at the end of the year. He found that even the leading steel manufacturers of Pittsburgh were completely unaware of whether they had made a profit or suffered a loss. Carnegie wanted to know whether he was making or losing money before the end of the year.

He developed a system that could account for every penny—one that would weigh the materials they were using and note what they were collecting or spending. This system was slowly introduced, and it allowed Carnegie and his partners to know how much money they were spending, what each worker was doing, who wasted material, who was able to save material, and, most importantly, who was able to make the best product.

This system was all well and good, but not too many mill managers liked it. After some time, however, Carnegie and his partners were able to keep tabs on all the activities of the workers in the steel mills. They were not only able to keep an eye on the activities of the department but also on every individual worker.

Carnegie noted that the key to being successful in whatever business you do is to have a flawless system for accounting so that you can keep track of any surplus, loss, wasted material, or saved material. Some steel manufacturers didn't trust secretaries and assistants with money unless there was some kind of account that allowed the manufacturer to keep track of the money, but they provided unchecked quantities of steel to the workers and did not check if the weight was the same when the men returned the steel in the form of finished products.

This really was a very inefficient method of running a steel business or any business for that matter. To have a successful business, one must keep track of everything.

Carnegie's steel business used the Siemens gas furnace to heat the iron. The cost, however, was great, and older and more conventional steel manufacturers were opposed to the amount of money that Carnegie and his partners were spending on melting metal. The benefit of using these furnaces, however, was that they could reduce the amount of material that was wasted.

It would be several years until other producers started following in the footsteps of Carnegie's steel business and paid dearly to melt their iron.

Because Carnegie and his partners had a well-working system in their firm that allowed them to keep track of everything and also watch how much metal was being wasted when it was melted in large quantities, they met a man by the name of William Borntraeger. He was a distant relative of Andrew Kloman and a simple clerk. He had drawn up a detailed assessment showing what the results of Carnegie's firm would be for a certain period of time. Carnegie and his partners were very impressed with his man's initiative and work, and Mr. Borntraeger was promoted to superintendent of the works. He later became a partner of Carnegie, and he was living like a millionaire by the time he died.

Chapter 9 Oil Interest

Carnegie's interest in oil surfaced in 1862 thanks to the oil wells of Pennsylvania. A friend of Carnegie's, one Mr. William Coleman, was interested in the oil wells there, and Carnegie went with him to see them.

Many others had also gone to the oil wells, hoping to make a fortune. There weren't enough lodging spaces for everyone, but many were able to camp out. Although the area has been portrayed in history as dirty and chaotic, according to Carnegie, it was tranquil. Everyone was happy, laughing, and having a good time.

On the banks of streams, people were drilling for oil, their derricks rising one after the other, and chanting, in Carnegie's opinion rather strange mottoes. One of these was "Hell or China," referring to hitting oil but not stopping even if they hit hell or reached the other side of the world, which they thought was China.

Carnegie noted that Americans worked at a much faster pace than the British. Americans could very quickly establish a civilization, but the British would only be done verifying the legitimacy of a certain man to rise to the position of leader based on the status of his ancestors.

In other words, Carnegie was praising this land where everyone was equal to make his way and find his fortune. In his experience back in Scotland, Britain was a place that divided the gentry from the plebs. This kept a perpetual heel on the rise of any man.

It is from here, where Carnegie visited, that the outskirts of Oil Creek grew, and the city that formed around the oil industry was Titusville, just four miles to the south.

Not too long before crude oil was first harvested by Edwin Drake in Titusville it was already coming out of the ground. It seeped into Oil Creek, mixing with the water. Oil was prevalent in many places in the area and could be found in salt wells and water wells, contaminating the water. You could see it flowing in creeks and streams. In the beginning, it was more of a nuisance than a blessing. It was dirty, toxic, and difficult to clean. Nonetheless, it would be considered black gold.

The Seneca natives had a variety of uses for this oil. They used it to paint themselves when going to war, and they used it as medicine albeit ineffectively as a form of a disinfectant for the skin. The Indians harvested the oil by placing blankets or pieces of fabric in the running water in the creek and let them soak it up. They then took the blankets or pieces of cloth to squeeze out the oil.

Around 1850, one Mr. Samuel Kier collected the oil found in the salt wells that his father owned and bottled it. They were half-pints that Samuel sold as medicine, calling it Kier's Rock Oil. It was supposed to cure bronchitis and liver problems, but, of course, it didn't.

The oil also had other uses. It was used to light lamps, but the primary source of flame at the time was whale oil. Whale blubber was rendered and shipped throughout the country, but the demand was so great that whalers were not able to keep up with it. This made it expensive, and only the wealthy could afford such luxuries and light their homes at night. The rest of the people, such as farmers and villagers and the poor in the city, were forced to go without light until morning.

Although there were other ways of lighting their homes, as with tallow (derived from animals) and coal oil (derived from shale), these were also expensive as was the process of extraction, and the oil supply was limited. Other forms of oil that could be used included cottonseed oil and lard oil, but these were not affordable and also not convenient to use. A replacement was necessary, and those who could solve the problem would be paid handsomely. Electricity and the light bulb were still a long way off.

Along came Mr. George Bissell, who had graduated from Dartmouth College and worked as a school principal, a professor of Greek language, a lawyer, and a journalist. In his spare time, he was also an inventor. Sometime in the 1850s, he had an idea for a new way to fuel the lights in people's homes. He thought that perhaps the oil that had been found in the western regions of Pennsylvania could be a better fuel for lamps.

He founded the Pennsylvania Rock Oil Company and sent a small amount of the oil to a Mr. Benjamin Silliman Jr., a professor of chemistry at Yale University. In 1855, Mr. Silliman concluded that Bissell's suspicions were true and that rock oil could be processed to be fuel for lamps.

Now that it was possible, the Pennsylvania Rock Oil Company faced a different problem. They had to gather large amounts of oil. Practically no infrastructure had been built around oil exploration. All they had were streams and creeks with traces of oil, and this looked like a contaminant rather than an asset. They figured that it came from the ground, so it was logical to look for underground oil deposits. Near the end of 1857, close to three years after Silliman corroborated Bissell's suspicions, explorers were commissioned to look for large deposits of oil. Today, there is a body of science and rational thought in the field of exploration, which is a billion dollar business, but back then it was anybody's guess. At this point, Bissell's company had been renamed Seneca Oil Company in tribute to the Seneca tribe.

It was thanks to a Mr. Townsend, a banker in New Haven who helped finance this exploration mission, that someone was able to search for large deposits of oil. He sent Mr. Edwin Drake, a man in his late thirties who suffered from a constant back problem. Mr. Drake was eventually given the title of colonel and dispatched to Titusville, Pennsylvania, in December 1857.

At this time, Oil Creek Valley, situated in Titusville, was not very sophisticated or modern. It was still densely packed with thick forests of hemlock and pine trees and the usual wildlife. These were harsh conditions to search for oil when you consider the dense forest and the lack of expertise in finding something below ground. Pipes had to be brought in, and hauling all the equipment was not easy. The people of Oil Creek liked Drake but thought he was wasting his time. It was impossible to think that there were any deposits of this toxic material.

He used the same kind of methods to find oil deposits that salt miners used in the salt mines. This was the first use of derricks to explore for oil. Back then the derricks were made of wood and towered ten to thirty feet above the ground where they bore into the earth.

Finally, after a long period of time, Drake succeeded in finding a well that contained this heavy, sludge-like material.

On Saturday, August 27, 1859, almost one and a half years after arriving in Oil Creek, Colonel Drake struck oil. It had now been proven that oil did exist in certain pockets beneath the ground, and his method was viable and effective. He now had a system that could be replicated and be the key to future success.

News of his find spread, and before long there was a rush to settle in Titusville. More derricks were set up, and more holes were bored to tap that well. They only had crude oil, and not much could be done with it, as it needed to be refined.

This led to the refining of the toxic sludge. To process the crude oil, many refineries were set up by independent companies to process the oil that was coming from independent drillers.

In less than a year after Drake struck oil, a large number of refineries had been set up in Oil Creek, but they were unable to extract usable heating oil to any profitable degree. Their methods were crude, and their output was low, but it was better than nothing. A lot of sludge was discarded in streams and the ground after the refining process, but most of it was sill heavy with usable hydrocarbons.

The Titusville Oil Creek area had begun by producing meager quantities of oil but was eventually able to produce enough to grow, expand, and thrive.

In the beginning, though, everything was run poorly, as expected. Barrels of oil were loaded into boats that were not very fit for sea anymore. The people who had begun to sell oil from Oil Creek had placed dams in some places in the creek, and when the time was just right, the dams were opened and the water was used to push the boats all the way down the creek, and they were able to float their way along the Allegheny River and finally reach Pittsburgh.

This method of transportation was inefficient and ineffective. Large quantities of oil were lost, and the waters on which they were transported were polluted with crude oil. Two-thirds of the original quantity of oil was lost, one-third having been lost during the time in which the people of Oil Creek were waiting to open the dams and the other third during transportation.

The oil that reached Pittsburgh was bottled and sold at rather high prices, and it was said to be excellent medicine, curing rheumatic problems. The oil was sold at one dollar per vial. As more oil became available, the price dropped and became very cheap.

The most popular wells at the time were on Storey farm. It was offered for sale at $45,000, and Carnegie and his partners bought it. Mr. William Coleman proposed to store 100,000 barrels of oil in the ground. To make up for the losses that would occur from leaks, oil was to be kept constantly flowing into the pool so that when the supply of oil was gone, Carnegie and his partners could sell their bounty and make a nice profit. This was one of the first instances of stockpiling. This day never came, however, and after having lost a great deal of oil, Carnegie and his partners abandoned the plan and did not continue to pool it.

The money made from the oil well from Storey farm was critical to Carnegie's overall success later in life. It had allowed for the construction of a brand-new steel mill in Pittsburgh, which called for all the money that Carnegie and his partners could raise to leverage their credit. From the start, Carnegie's credit was on solid footing, and he made sure it never faulted. He paid his loans on time and more often than not ahead of time. In this respect, he was much like Rockefeller, who valued his credit standing with the banks.

The next venture into the oil business was again with Mr. William Coleman and one Mr. David Ritchie. This oil field was in Ohio, and the oil there was an excellent lubricant. In 1864, Carnegie, Mr. Coleman, and Mr. Ritchie visited the oil field and purchased it.

The journey to the oil field was fine, but the trip back was rather uncomfortable. During the return journey, torrential rains fell, and the carriage in which they were riding started to rock back and forth as it sunk and climbed out of soft spots in the ground where the road had been soaked.

The two men who rode with him were rather portly, while Carnegie himself at that time was rather thin. He was squeezed between them, and they rocked back and forth as the carriage made its way in and out of potholes. Despite the discomfort of the trip, Carnegie and his companions were elated by the business they had just concluded.

They reached a small town the following night. They had seen the church in town and heard its bell toll. When they eventually arrived, it coincided with the arrival of a minister the town was waiting for. The minister was delayed, however, due to the heavy rains, and the townspeople mistook Carnegie for the minister.

The welcoming party asked Carnegie and his partners when they would be ready to enter the meetinghouse. Carnegie, Mr. Ritchie, and Mr. Coleman were all tempted to accept, finding it amusing, but Carnegie was so exhausted that he just could not do it. As Carnegie later noted, that was the closest he ever got to give a speech at a church podium.

After some time, Carnegie found that his business affairs required much of his time and attention and realized that he needed to quit his job at the Pennsylvania Railroad Company. Shortly before Carnegie resigned, he was invited to meet with the president of the Pennsylvania Railroad, Mr. John Edgar Thomson, who was going to promote Carnegie to the position of assistant general superintendent. If Carnegie took the job, he was going to have his office in Altoona, the city where he had stayed with Mr. Scott several years earlier before becoming superintendent of the Pittsburgh Division.

Carnegie refused the offer, saying that he was planning to leave the company and make a great fortune for himself. He said that he did not see how he could accomplish his goal if he continued to work for a paycheck.

On March 28, 1865, Andrew Carnegie resigned from the Pennsylvania Railroad Company. As a gift, the railwaymen presented him with a gold watch. Earlier, President Thomson had written a letter to Carnegie congratulating him on his resignation from the Pennsylvania Railroad. Carnegie took this letter and really cherished his gold watch.

Leaving was a subject of great consternation for Carnegie. No doubt he wanted to pursue his own path, but it was a path that would have its pitfalls and be harder to traverse. Staying at the railroad at such a high position and with the possibility of taking the top spot one day not being too far out of the question would have been tempting for any man, but he knew he had to move on. There was more to explore, more to conquer, and more to do.

He wrote a heartfelt letter of resignation in which he described his dozen years at Pennsylvania Railroad with deep fondness. He had, after all, started at the lowest rung of the ladder and worked his way up to the second highest-paying job in the company. He had learned so much. It had become the foundation of his eventual steel empire. The knowledge he gained from taking care of problems and how to fix them gave him insight into many opportunities, ranging from sleeper cars to carriages to railway lines and bridges. Now he wanted more.

Carnegie left his job at the Pennsylvania Railroad Company and set out to earn his fortune from simply his businesses. He was not going to earn money by working for a paycheck.

Carnegie has said that one needs to be in a service where they answer to superiors. He notes that even leaders and presidents are bombarded with different advice and suggestions, are forced to do certain things, and have very little independence.

Two years after he retired from the Pennsylvania Railroad Company, Carnegie, his friend Henry Phipps, and a certain J.W. Vandevort toured through Europe, particularly in Scotland, Carnegie's home, and England. Vandevort had become "Vandy" between Carnegie and himself, and the two had become traveling buddies.

One Sunday when Carnegie and Vandevort were spending their time in the grass of a field, Carnegie asked, "If you could make $3,000, would you spend it on a tour through Europe with me?"

Vandevort responded by saying, "Would a duck swim or an Irishman eat potatoes?"

That $3,000 was acquired soon afterward in oil stock. Vandevort had invested in the oil stock with just a few hundred dollars he had in store. After that, Carnegie, Vandy, and Henry Phipps, or Harry, set out on a tour of Europe. They visited different capital cities, climbed spires, and even slept on mountaintops. They carried their luggage in knapsacks.

The end of their holiday was at Vesuvius, where they made the solemn promise to one day go around the world.

Carnegie's trip in Europe was, in his own opinion, very good for him. Before then he had not heard of art, particularly sculpting and painting. After his travels, however, he was able to categorize paintings of the masters. He felt that after visiting Europe and truly experiencing beautiful works of art and many other things that so much in America just seemed tasteless. What seemed magnificent before he had left the U.S. he now rejected.

He had strong beliefs that for one to succeed one needs to have a strong mind. This comes from a diversity of experience and thought. That diversity can only be achieved by travel.

Carnegie was already familiar with music, but he was truly affected during his trip to Europe. He had listened to the music of the Handel anniversary, which was being celebrated in the Crystal Palace in London. He had heard the music in cathedrals and the songs sung by the Pope's choir in Rome. All the music that he had listened to during his trip in Europe was really wonderful, empowering, and grand. It was part of the reason why his later endowments went to Carnegie Hall. It was just one way to get others to experience what he had experienced within his heart and how that experience had touched his soul.

Carnegie also found that after leaving the fast pace of the New World that the U.S. was moving too quickly, while countries in the rest of the world were comparatively much slower in progress.

The United States was zipping along like a fast car. There was good to this and bad. The race for prosperity and the pursuit of happiness had gained momentum, but the race for a more mindful and spiritual experience had been left aside as its cost. This was Carnegie's perspective. There was an enlightened side to Carnegie that permeated much of the thinking and reflection when he was older.

Advancing the Oil Wells

As previously mentioned, George Lauder, "Dod," had taken Mr. William Coleman to Wigan, England. There he showed Coleman how they washed the waste from the coal mines and extracted coke. Coleman had always been pressing Carnegie and his partners about the potential of using this supposed waste that was being discarded from the coal mines. Even disposing of the dross was quite expensive, and there would be another way.

Carnegie had great confidence in his cousin, and when he accepted what Coleman was telling them, he immediately started to get other coal companies to send them their dross. A ten-year contract was made with several prominent coal companies and several railway companies for transportation. Carnegie also put together the money to set up shops along the Pennsylvania Railroad.

Dod came to Pittsburgh to watch over everything, and he oversaw the construction of the first coal-washing device in the nation. His project was a success, as all his projects in the area were. It didn't take long before the money that was spent to set up everything and to build the machines was made back. Lauder's invention proved very useful for Carnegie's business, and Lauder became rather famous.

In time, many more Lauder machines were built until Carnegie had 500 of them washing close to 1,500 tons of coal every day. Carnegie was so impressed with all of this that he noted Lauder's genius

His point was that someone who could turn what was considered worthless junk and thrown away into something useful and meaningful was worth praise and admiration.

Another person who became a partner of Carnegie was the son of Carnegie's other cousin, Robert Morrison of Dunfermline. Robert, or Bob, had a son who had become the superintendent of one of the shops of Carnegie's coal business. He asked Carnegie if he knew of a mechanic who was exceptionally skillful and also one of his relatives. Carnegie said no and asked if he might speak to the superintendent.

When they began to talk, Carnegie asked him what his name was, and he replied, "Morrison, son of Robert." "Well, how did you come here?" Carnegie asked. "I thought we could better ourselves," he replied. "Who have you with you?" asked Carnegie. "My wife," he answered. "Why didn't you come first to see your relative who might have been able to introduce you here?" Carnegie asked. "Well, I didn't feel I needed help if I only got a chance", replied Morrison.

That was a classic trait of a Morrison—always very independent. He had been promoted to the position of superintendent of one of the shops in

Duquesne. From there he continued to rise in position. In Carnegie's old days, Morrison, still seemingly young, had become a millionaire but still retained his humility.

Carnegie always suggested that he and his partners should expand the business into making steel and iron. Steel manufacturers were not yet very popular in America, and they were concerned that America was importing too much from other countries. That changed through government intervention after the Civil War. Tariffs were placed on imports, and the fear of steel manufacturers evaporated. The Civil War caused people to want to rely only on their own country and to make everything they vitally needed. In the past, the United States had no choice but to buy steel from other countries, largely Britain, the country that had secretly supported the Confederacy during the war. It became a national strategic imperative that critical resources be allowed to prosper.

American citizens wanted nothing more than for their country to produce their own goods. Congress then presented manufacturers with a tariff of 28 percent on steel rails. Thus, for every ton of steel rails bought from outside, 28 percent of the original price was added to that price.

This policy of making their own materials and goods allowed the manufacturing business in general in the United States to flourish. Before the Civil War, this policy was not firmly pressed, and the South and the North differed on it. Southerners viewed it as a policy convenient only for the North, while they stood for free trade. Since the British government had supported the South during the Civil War, Northerners disliked them. The policy of protection was then agreed to by both Southerners and Northerners, and producing your own goods became a patriotic activity after the war.

Many no longer thought twice about venturing into the business of manufacturing. They were sure they were safe. Long after the Civil War ended, people began to call for the tariff on foreign imports to be reduced. In the beginning, this did not happen, and people suspected that some manufacturers were bribing congressmen to keep the tariff so that they could continue to make and sell their products. In truth, however, manufacturers were raising just enough money every year to run the Iron and Steel Association.

Tariffs on steel were eventually reduced, and thanks to Carnegie sometimes dropped to only $7 per ton.

In 1911, the tariff dropped a further ½%.

When Grover Cleveland was president of the United States, he wanted a tariff that was very impractical. His tariff would be a severe blow to many manufacturers making several different products. When this issue came about, Carnegie was summoned to Washington, where he tried to improve what was called the Wilson Bill. Carnegie, Governor Flower of New York, Senator

Gorman, and several other Democrats sided with Carnegie and opposed the Wilson Bill. Several of those who stood with Carnegie believed that the Wilson Bill would inevitably damage the nation's manufacturing industry.

Carnegie was given the responsibility of suggesting a lower tariff by Flower, Gorman, and the other protectionist Democrats. He came up with a certain tariff that all of them agreed on, which was called the Wilson-Gorman Tariff Bill. Later, Gorman told Carnegie that he had to be lenient regarding cotton ties to gain Southern senators as supporters for keeping protection intact.

Carnegie's role in the tariffs on imported foods was, conversely, to try to reduce the tariffs. He did not support those who wanted higher taxes paid for imported goods, and neither did he support those who wanted no taxes on imported goods. He stood in the middle, supporting taxes that were reasonable but high enough to keep manufacturing intact. The point of balance that

Carnegie straddled was one where the tariffs would help local manufacturers compete, and the people would have inexpensive access to goods and services. Raising tariffs of external suppliers sometimes had the effect of raising the prices of local goods, which meant that the consumer paid the price. Besides, pure competition of goods would also serve as an incentive to develop better technologies.

By 1907, all tariffs placed on steel and iron were able to be dropped. By this time, manufacturing in the United States had already prospered so much that even if someone bought goods from other countries it wouldn't hurt the firms. In the infancy of manufacturing, however, it was extremely important that everyone bought from the manufacturers in the country instead of fattening the wallets of outside manufacturers.

Europe did not produce much, and thus prices there were very expensive. This was another reason why it was all right for the tariffs to be dropped, for very few people would pay so much for so little, as prices in Europe were quite high.

The only "negative" effect that free trade had on manufacturers was that there couldn't be high prices on their products. Other than that, everything was secure. Carnegie himself said this to an audience at the Tariff Commission in Washington in 1910.

Chapter 10 New York

As the steel and oil business of Carnegie and his partners grew, it became necessary for him to regularly travel to the East and most often to New York, where all large businesses had their headquarters. Carnegie said that New York was the equivalent of London, and that no company could ever hope to do well unless it had a stronghold in New York.

He traveled to New York so often that he eventually moved there.

Carnegie's brother, Thomas, had already married Lucy Coleman, daughter of Mr. William Coleman, who had worked with Carnegie and his partners for some time and was a companion at the beginning of the oil industry. Carnegie's home in Homewood was given to Thomas, and Carnegie left for New York with his mother, who wanted to go with him. Although they were happy as long as they were together, Carnegie's mother still felt sad to leave Pittsburgh again.

When the family had moved to Altoona when Mr. Scott became superintendent of the Pittsburgh Division for the Pennsylvania Railroad, friendships were cut and relationships ended. Now they had to leave Pittsburgh again to a place totally alien to them.

When Carnegie and his mother arrived in New York, they lived at the St. Nicholas Hotel, and he took an office on Broad Street.

At the beginning of their stay in New York, they were most happy when friends from Pittsburgh visited them. Carnegie and his mother also traveled to Pittsburgh to maintain the friendships.

After some time, however, New York began to feel like home, and they made friends there too. Later, the Windsor Hotel, which was also owned by the owners of the St. Nicholas, opened, and Carnegie and his mother spent their lives there until 1887. They lived solely in these two hotels for twenty years!

The owner of the hotel, Mr. Hawk, became a close friend of Carnegie as did his son and nephew.

Carnegie has noted that he gained many educational benefits in New York, most important being the Nineteenth Century Club founded by the Palmers. Mr. and Mrs. Courtlandt Palmer's club was meant to bring together people every month to talk about various subjects. It was thanks to a certain Madame Botta that Carnegie became a member. She was the wife of Professor Botta, and he was once invited to dine with them. At the meal, he met several other people of high status, and one of them was a certain Mr. Andrew D. White, who went on to become Carnegie's counselor and friend.

At the time, however, White was president of Cornell University and later became ambassador to both Russia and Germany.

At each gathering of the members of the Nineteenth Century Club, men and women gave speeches about the most talked about topics of the day. Soon, the number of attendees grew so large that the meeting could no longer be held in a private room. They were subsequently held at the American Art Galleries.

Carnegie once spoke on the topic "The Aristocracy of the Dollar."

He thought his speaking was excellent, for in order to speak, he had to learn, and he loved learning things.

While in Pittsburgh, Carnegie had found that only a few businesses and businessmen dealt with the New York Stock Exchange, and the Oil and Stock Exchange in Pittsburgh did not exist at that time. Pittsburgh was a manufacturing city.

Carnegie found that New York was quite different, and nearly all businessmen there were involved with the New York Stock Exchange.

Carnegie was constantly approached with questions regarding his dealings with railway ventures. He was also invited to a party where the hosts were intending to buy certain properties, but Carnegie never attended or paid attention to these men.

One of the most important offers he ever received, however, was from a Mr. Jay Gould, who spoke to Carnegie at the Windsor Hotel. This was the same Jay Gould who had crossed Cornelius Vanderbilt. He told Carnegie that he wanted to buy the controlling interests of the Pennsylvania Railroad Company. He wanted Carnegie to manage the company, and he would receive 50 percent of the profits. Carnegie thanked him but declined the offer, saying that he was a close friend of Mr. Scott.

Shortly afterward, Mr. Scott and Carnegie met, and Mr. Scott told him that he had learned that Carnegie had been chosen by several people in New York to become the next president of the Pennsylvania Railroad after himself. Carnegie did not know how Mr. Scott had known about this, for Carnegie had never even said a word of it to him. Carnegie assured Mr. Scott that he would not be the president of any railroad company other than one he had founded.

About thirty years after Mr. Gould made his offer to Carnegie, Carnegie spoke to Mr. Gould's son and told him about the offer his father had presented to him. He said, "Your father offered me control of the great Pennsylvania system. Now I offer his son in return the control of an international line from ocean to ocean."

Carnegie and Mr. Gould's son decided they would first bring the Wabash line to Pittsburgh. Everything went well, and the contract made with the Wabash was that one-third of the business that Carnegie's steel business received was to be given to the Wabash.

Just before Carnegie and Mr. Gould's son were about to expand in the East from Pittsburgh all the way to the Atlantic, a certain Mr. Schwab talked to Carnegie on behalf of Mr. Morgan. Carnegie was asked whether or not he was actually going to retire from business. Carnegie replied that he was, which would be the end of railway ventures for Carnegie and his partners.

Carnegie really only bought a small number of shares of the Pennsylvania Railroad Company when he was very young, and he had done so for the purpose of investment. Carnegie did not pay for the shares because bankers were willing to carry his shares for him for a small price. Carnegie did, however, buy a few shares of companies he did not really get involved in.

Carnegie had a very strict rule. He was not going to buy what he didn't pay for, and he wasn't going to sell what wasn't his to sell.

When Carnegie owned stocks and shares, he wanted to know what the stocks were quoted at in the newspaper. He went on to sell the shares he owned that were part of other companies, and he turned his entire attention to his own business. Carnegie also made it a point that he would not buy or even own a stock that was sold on a stock exchange.

For the most part, he stood by this principle.

Carnegie believed that this principle should be followed by all businessmen. Carnegie has said that this is especially important for a man in the manufacturing industry. In his opinion, it leaves a man distracted and always thinking about his shares. This would wreck his judgment, something that is needed in the business of manufacturing, which requires you to think about a problem calmly. If he is already anxious about his shares, he would not be able to think right and would end up making a reckless or careless decision.

The most meaningful venture that Carnegie undertook in New York was building a bridge across the Mississippi River at Keokuk. Edgar Thomson, who was then still president of the Pennsylvania Railroad, worked with Carnegie for the bridge. Carnegie and Mr. Edgar Thomson were willing to accept stocks and bonds as payment for their work.

Everything went well except monetarily. Thanks to a crisis that occurred, the company that had contracted for Carnegie to build their bridge went bankrupt and was unable to pay Carnegie his fee. In turn, a rival bridge-building concern took up the job and built a bridge across the Mississippi at Burlington. They also built a railway line that ran along the western bank of the Mississippi all the way to Keokuk.

Thomson and Carnegie were never able to receive their profits, but at least they did not suffer a loss.

The bridge that Carnegie had taken up the contract to build was built in the shops of the Keystone Works in Pittsburgh. The project called for Carnegie to frequently visit Keokuk.

These visits permitted Carnegie to meet General Reid and his wife. The English people, in Carnegie's opinion, considered the people of the Far West in the United States to be barely civilized. These people were friends of Carnegie's and well received by Mr. and Mrs. Reid at an impressive gathering in Britain.

Carnegie became so famous for building the Keokuk bridge that he was approached by several people who were entrusted with building the Mississippi bridge at St. Louis. In 1869, Carnegie was approached by a Mr. Macpherson. He was from Scotland and told Carnegie that he was trying to acquire the necessary funds to build the bridge. He was inquiring if Carnegie would be able to get a few of the Eastern railway companies to build it.

After considering it, Carnegie drew up the contract for constructing the bridge to be done by the Keystone Bridge Works. Carnegie was also able to sell $4 million worth of shares of the Keystone Bridge Company. He then set off for

London in March 1869 to negotiate the sale of the bonds.

During Carnegie's trip to London, he drew up a description of what was happening. After arriving in London, Carnegie met with Junius S. Morgan, a prominent banker at the time and the father of J.P. Morgan. Carnegie conducted negotiations with him and furnished him with a copy of the prospectus he had made. He was informed the next day that Morgan was positive about the matter. Carnegie sold a portion of the shares to Morgan and said that the rest of the shares were also available. Morgan's lawyers, however, proposed different terms. When Carnegie heard those terms, he made a counter proposal to which Morgan had to revert to his lawyers for advice.

Morgan tried to get Carnegie to go off to Scotland, as he was planning to go there. He said that everything could be ready by the time he returned in three weeks, but Carnegie had no intention of leaving matters hanging in midair while he was away. He responded by saying that he would have a telegram delivered the following morning that stipulated his agreement to the changes. The Atlantic telegram line had already been open for some time, but it wasn't certain if the line would be able to carry a message that was as long as he was writing. He put in the message all the changes and all the official statements and showed it to Mr. Morgan before he sent it. After seeing it, he said, "Well, young man, if you succeed in that you deserve a red mark."

When Carnegie entered the office the following morning, he had a letter from Mr. Morgan's private office. It was the answer to Carnegie's changes: "Board meeting last night; changes all approved." After seeing the answer, Carnegie said to Mr. Morgan, "Now, Mr. Morgan, we can proceed, assuming that the bond is as your lawyers desire."

Shortly afterward, the matter was settled.

During the time that Carnegie was in the office of Junius Spencer Morgan while he was still in London, he was approached by a man by the name of Mr. Sampson, who was at the time the financial editor for The Times. The two men met in Mr. Sampson's office.

Carnegie understood that speaking to him would mean that the price of the bonds that were on the Stock Exchange would rise.

Carnegie talked about Fisk and Gould and spoke of how the St. Louis Bridge Company was related to the national government. Mr. Sampson said he would be happy to place this information in *The Times*. Mr. Sampson left the office, and Morgan then slapped Carnegie on the shoulder and said, "Thank you, young man; you have raised the price of those bonds 5 percent this morning." Carnegie responded by saying, "All right, Mr. Morgan, now show me how I can raise them 5 percent more for you."

Everything went well, and Carnegie was able to acquire the funds necessary to build the St. Louis bridge. This whole affair was Carnegie's first time engaging with European bankers.

Later, a certain Mr. Pullman met with Carnegie and told him that Mr. Morgan had said at a dinner party, "That young man will be heard from." That "young man" was Andrew Carnegie.

After finishing his business with J.S. Morgan, Carnegie took a trip to Dunfermline, his hometown. There he presented to the city public baths as a gift. It was the first real gift Carnegie had made to his hometown. Many years earlier when Carnegie was in the telegram business, his Uncle Lauder had suggested to Carnegie that he subscribe to the Wallace Monument, which was being built on Stirling Heights.

At the time, Carnegie was earning a mere $30 a month, and paying for the seemingly small expense of the subscription was very expensive for a man earning such a salary. Carnegie's mother was not upset about it and was very happy to see that her son's name was listed as someone who had contributed.

Many years later, Carnegie and his mother visited the Wallace Monument in Stirling, and there she presented to the monument committee a bust of Sir Walter Scott.

By this time, Carnegie and his mother were in a much better financial situation, although Carnegie was not yet giving money. He was at the time in accumulation and saving mode.

While Carnegie was on his trip to Europe with his friends Vandy and Harry, he was not completely relaxed. He was always thinking about business.

Letters were regularly sent to him to keep him informed about matters at home. During Carnegie's excursion in Europe, the construction of a railway line to the Pacific was considered, and the United States Congress passed an act that encouraged construction of the line. While Carnegie was in Rome, he realized that this line could be completed long before it was expected to be. Carnegie then wrote Mr. Scott and told him that they could place sleeping cars on the California railway. Mr. Scott responded, "Well, young man, you do take time by the forelock." This was also his reaction when Carnegie had approached him many years earlier when the sleeping car was first thought of by inventor Theodore Tuttle Woodruff.

Despite Mr. Scott's unsatisfactory reply, Carnegie went on with his plans after returning to the United States.

The demand for sleeping cars was so high that it was hard to produce enough to meet the demand. This led to the founding of the Pullman Company by George Pullman. At the time, the Central Transportation Company was not able to meet the demand for the sleeping car, and Pullman very soon became a competitor.

He chose Chicago as the place to start, which was the largest railway center in the nation at that time.

When the president of the Union Pacific Railway was once in Chicago, Pullman met with him. Pullman waited in the office for the railway president, and while there he saw a telegram addressed to Mr. Scott. It read, "Your proposition for sleeping cars is accepted." Later, when Mr. Durrant, president of the Union Pacific, came into the office, Pullman spoke to him about how he had read the telegram and said, "I trust you not decide this matter until I have made a proposition to you."

The railway president agreed to hear what Pullman had to say.

A board meeting of the Union Pacific Railway was held in New York not long afterward. Both Pullman and Carnegie attended the meeting, both eager to be given the responsibility of building sleeping cars.

Carnegie and Pullman met there, and Carnegie said, "Good evening, Mr. Pullman! Here we are together, and are we not making a nice couple of fools of ourselves?" Mr. Pullman asked, "What do you mean?"

The problem was actually quite simple. Carnegie explained that because of their competing for the job at hand they were losing. Pullman responded, "Well, what do you propose to do about it?" Carnegie replied, "Unite. Make a joint proposition to the Union Pacific, your party and mine, and organize a company." Pullman then asked, "What would you call it?" Carnegie responded, "The Pullman Palace Car Company." This name gelled well with both of them, and Pullman invited Carnegie to his room to discuss the matter.

Everything went well, and they were given the contract. Carnegie's company was joined with Pullman's, and Carnegie and his partners held shares of Pullman's company.

In 1873, a financial crisis came crashing down, and Carnegie was forced to sell his shares in Pullman's company to save his own steel business. Carnegie believed that he was the biggest shareholder in the company until he had to sell his shares.

George Pullman was at first a carpenter, and his first major venture was when a house in Chicago had to be elevated.
Slowly, he became a well-known contractor in the business of elevating houses.

Pullman was so skilled in this line of work that if a hotel needed to be raised by ten feet he could do it without disrupting the business of the hotel or be an inconvenience to the several hundred people staying in the hotel.

Mr. Pullman was a very fast-paced man and saw, as Carnegie did, the necessity for having sleeping cars on the lines. He began constructing sleeping cars after being awarded contracts by different railway companies.

The Eastern Company and Mr. T.T. Woodruff were the real owners of the patents for the sleeping car, and this issue caused a bit of trouble for Pullman.

Carnegie suggested that Pullman's firm and the Eastern Company should merge. This was exactly the same course of action he himself had taken earlier when his company and Pullman's were trying to get the contract to build sleeping cars.

Carnegie decided to fix everything himself, seeing that the relationship between him, Pullman, and the Eastern Company was on good terms, whereas Pullman's relationship with the Eastern Company was rather awkward.

Everything went well, and the Central Transportation Company was joined with the Pullman Company, allowing Pullman to extend his range of activities into the East. Pullman was given control of the Pennsylvania trunk line to the Atlantic.

Carnegie observed that Pullman was a very determined person. He had problems at times as everyone does and sometimes never performed at his best but was determined to do his best.

Pullman once told Carnegie a story about an old man from the West who had suffered a great many illnesses, and one day when he was being spoken to by his neighbors in a most sympathetic tone, he replied, "Yes, my friends, all that you say is true. I have had a long, long life full of troubles, but there is one curious fact about them—nine-tenths of them never happened."

The moral of that story is that the better part of one's problems are created in your mind and don't exist in the real world. One may feel that it is real, but that is because it is conjured in the mind. These imaginary issues should simply be brushed aside.

Carnegie was doing very well at the time and soon attracted the attention of other firms. In 1871, he was approached by the Union Pacific

Railway that needed his help to raise $600,000 to keep the company up and running until the problem they were in was over.

He was also told by his friends who worked for Union Pacific that he would be able to raise the funds necessary, and that he could even give the Pennsylvania Railroad control of the Western line, an important railway.

Carnegie decided that he would do it. He traveled to Philadelphia to speak with President Edgar Thomson of the Pennsylvania Railroad. Carnegie thought that if the Union Pacific was fine with having a few Pennsylvania Railroad men on their board, the business the Pennsylvania Railroad would receive would be a proper reason to help the Union Pacific.

When Carnegie met with Mr. Thomson, he said that if he were to be given the securities regarding the money of the Pennsylvania Railroad and have the Union Pacific borrow their money up in New York, then the

Pennsylvania Railroad would be able to control the Union Pacific and use it to its advantage. Carnegie has described President Thomson as a man who cared more for the company's money than his own. He spent his own money freely but was very particular about the expenditures of the Pennsylvania Railroad.

If the whole job were to come crashing down and if the $600,000 were to disappear, the Pennsylvania Railroad wouldn't really suffer a blow. It had already been agreed upon that if the job failed President Thomson would be given the securities of the Union Pacific that Carnegie now had for giving the loan to the Union Pacific Railway.

The meeting between Carnegie and President Thomson took place at his home in Philadelphia, and just when they had finished their talk and Carnegie was about to leave, Thomson put his hand on Carnegie's shoulder and said, "Remember, Andy, I look to you in this matter. It is you I trust, and I depend on your holding all the securities you obtain and seeing that the Pennsylvania Railroad is never in a position where it can lose a dollar."

This basically meant that President Thomson trusted Carnegie and placed him in charge of keeping the Pennsylvania Railroad's funds intact. Carnegie went on with his job, and everything turned out well.

When all was practically said and done, the Union Pacific was not too comfortable with having the president of the Pennsylvania Railroad as their president as well. Thomson resolutely put down the proposition, and he went on to appoint Thomas A. Scott vice president of the Union Pacific Railway. As for Carnegie and Pullman, they were elected members of the board and took up the position of director. Mr. Scott, too, became a member of the board, and in 1871 all three men were members of the board of the Union Pacific Railway.

In return for securing the necessary funds for the Union Pacific, Carnegie was given $3 million in shares of the company. This payment was kept in Carnegie's safe. After what had happened between the Pennsylvania Railroad and the Union Pacific, the stock of the Union Pacific became much more valuable. It was at this time that Carnegie went off to London to discuss terms of some bonds for building a bridge across the Missouri River from Omaha.

Carnegie had left instructions with his secretary that Mr. Scott was to be allowed access to the safe, for he was part of the business of the Union Pacific. While Carnegie was away in London, Mr. Scott decided to sell the shares of the Union Pacific that he and Carnegie owned.

Carnegie had granted Mr. Scott access to the safe because aside from the fact that Mr. Scott was a business partner, Carnegie felt that the bonds should be within reach of one of his partners if he were away. Carnegie probably never considered that Mr. Scott might actually sell those bonds.

When Carnegie returned from London, he found that he was being pushed aside by the members of the Union Pacific Railroad. He had previously been treated as a partner, and now he was being treated like an outsider.

It was very rare that anyone could say they had worked with a firm as great as the Union Pacific, and now Mr. Scott had just sold their position away! This was the first issue in the relationship between Mr. Scott and Carnegie that caused a slight difference between them.

Both Carnegie and Pullman were not informed of Mr. Scott's decision, and both were quite upset with Mr. Scott's course of action. Pullman responded in a retaliatory manner and once again invested his profits in the shares of the company. Carnegie was very tempted to follow suit, but he understood that it would mean stooping to that level, and, more importantly, it would be unappreciative on his part to cut such a line between him and friend Mr. Scott.

Soon after the incident, Pullman, Mr. Scott, and Carnegie were kicked off the board. This was very difficult for Carnegie to accept, and it was the first thing that was really a dividing wall between him and Mr. Scott. Later, President Thomson of the Pennsylvania Railroad apologized for the incident and said that since the matter had been left in the hands of Carnegie and Mr. Scott, he concluded that Carnegie had thought that the best course of action was to sell the bonds.

After this regrettable incident with Union Pacific, Carnegie was anxious that he might lose a friend of his, a Mr. Levi P. Morton of Morton, Bliss, and Co. Mr. Morton was somewhat connected with Union Pacific, but after a time he found that Carnegie had nothing to do with selling the bonds.

The contract for the Omaha Bridge was secured, as the people who ordered the bridge had been in league with Union Pacific before Carnegie had ever joined the company. The talks conducted were with the people who ordered the bridge and not with Union Pacific.

Carnegie was unaware of this even though a director of Union Pacific had spoken with him before he left for London.

The negotiations resulted in the people who ordered the bridge purchasing two and a half million bonds.

What also went wrong when Carnegie returned to New York aside from the issue with Union Pacific was that his profit from the bonds and everyone else's, too, was taken by certain people, and they were used to settle their debts. Carnegie had to go without claiming his rightful profit, which was a rather large sum and made nothing for his efforts. He had been swindled out of his share.

Carnegie realized that he was actually still quite green and needed to learn more. He also learned that although most people are trustworthy and honest, you might want to keep an eye on some of them.

Shortly after the incident with Union Pacific, Carnegie was approached by Colonel William Philips, president of the Allegheny Valley Railway. Philips once went to Carnegie's office in New York and said he needed money, and that he could not get any bank in the nation to buy his five million bonds. The bonds were, however, assured by the Pennsylvania Railroad Company.

The bankers had only agreed to purchase them under their terms. He had priced the bonds at ninety cents each, which was considered ridiculously high by the bankers. At the time, bonds of Western railway companies were sold at eighty cents each. After telling him his problem, he wanted to know if Carnegie could help him.

Colonel Philips desperately needed $250,000, and no one was willing to give him that much money—not the banks and not even President Thomson of the Pennsylvania Railroad (the Pennsylvania). The bonds that Colonel Philips was trying to sell were not able to be paid for in gold—only in American dollars. This made the bonds unfit to be sold to outside banks or investors.

Carnegie knew that the Pennsylvania Railroad owned an impressive quantity of 6 percent gold bonds of the Philadelphia as well as the Erie Railroad Company. Carnegie thought about trading the Philadelphia and Erie bonds for the Allegheny Railway bonds that had an interest payment of 7 percent.

Carnegie contacted President Thomson and asked him if the Pennsylvania Railroad Company could lend $250,000 with interest to the Allegheny Railway.

President Thomson willingly agreed, and Colonel Philips was delighted. Philips offered Carnegie the opportunity of purchasing his five million bonds, each being priced at ninety cents. He gave Carnegie sixty days to give his answer.

Carnegie proposed a trade to President Thomson—a trade of the Allegheny Railway bonds in return for the Philadelphia and Erie Railroad bonds. Carnegie then went to London. After arriving at Queenstown, he contacted the Barings of another financial bank in Britain. Carnegie said that he was selling a security that they would most definitely want to purchase. Later, when Carnegie arrived in London, he found a note asking him to call the Barings.

Carnegie telephoned the Barings the following morning and met them shortly afterward. Carnegie was able to get everything in order, and the Barings were willing to purchase the bonds by the time the meeting was over. After the bank sold the bonds to an investor, a customer of theirs, they would subtract their fee from the amount and furnish the loan with 5 percent interest. Carnegie was bound to earn $500,000 in profit by the time everything was said and done.

The necessary paperwork had to be created, but just before Carnegie left the banking house, a certain Mr. Russell Sturgis stopped him and said that Mr. Baring himself was visiting London the following morning, and that they would wait to sign the papers in front of him. Carnegie was told to call at 2:00 the following afternoon.

Carnegie felt that he should telegraph President Thomson, although he had a nagging feeling that he should not. Something didn't feel right. He thus decided to do nothing at the moment and walked back to the Langham Hotel, where he was staying. When Carnegie arrived, he found a messenger waiting for him. The message was a not from the Barings. It was sealed and unopened.

Certain problems involving Chancellor Bismarck of Germany had caused problems for many people, and the Barings contacted Carnegie. They said they could not carry on with the plans and could not try to advise Mr. Baring into proceeding with them either.

The breaking of the deal had seemed so unlikely just a little while earlier, and now it had actually happened. Carnegie was not too disturbed by the breakup of the plans and was just happy that he did contact President Thomson to update him.

Carnegie did not go back to the Barings for this and instead turned to J.S. Morgan & Co., the bank of Junius S. Morgan. He did not go to Morgan at first, but the bank was dealing with several American issues, and Carnegie went to Morgan to complete his duty. In the end, the Philadelphia and Erie Railway bonds were sold to Morgan's bank for a cheaper price than what the Barings had agreed to.

Carnegie did not go straight to Morgan when he arrived in London because Mr. Philips of the Allegheny Railway had said he had already tried Morgan's banking house in the United States, and they did not take him up on his offer. Carnegie thus thought that the banking house of Morgan in London might also feel the same as their office in the States. Carnegie did, however, make it a point to always go first to Morgan. Whenever Carnegie had some proposition to offer, Morgan would try to take it up, but if he couldn't, he would get another bank that was not a competitor and tell Carnegie to go there.

One day Carnegie said to Mr. Morgan, "Mr. Morgan, I will give you an idea and help you to carry it forward if you will give me one-quarter of all the money you made by acting upon it." Morgan replied, "That seems fair, and as I have the option to act upon it, or not, certainly we ought to be willing to pay you a quarter of the profit."

Carnegie talked about how he had traded the Allegheny Railway bonds for the Philadelphia and Erie Railroad bonds. He also spoke of how the Pennsylvania Railroad was guaranteeing the Philadelphia and Erie Railroad bonds. Carnegie went on to say that if a good enough price was put up for the bonds the Pennsylvania might just sell them. At the time, everyone was buying American bonds, and Carnegie said that he could float the bonds. Morgan agreed to Carnegie's plan.

This would basically mean that the Pennsylvania Railroad would sell its Philadelphia and Erie Railroad bonds and make back the money it had loaned.

President Thomson of the Pennsylvania Railroad was then in Paris, and Carnegie met him there. He told him what he had spoken about with Mr. Morgan of J.S. Morgan & Co. Carnegie understood that the Pennsylvania Railroad always needed money, and that's why he knew this plan would work. Carnegie asked Thomson to name a price that Morgan would then place on the bonds. The price he presented was quite high for the time but still plausible. Morgan bought a portion of the bonds, and the Allegheny bonds were put up for sale, and the Pennsylvania Railroad Company was able to make back its money.

Unfortunately, not too many bonds were sold by the time the financial crisis of 1873 struck. At the time, Carnegie was receiving money from the bonds from the son of Junius S. Morgan, John Pierpont Morgan, also known as J.P. Morgan. One day John Morgan said to Carnegie, "My father has cabled to ask whether you wish to sell out your interest in that idea you gave him." Carnegie responded by saying, "Yes, I do. In these days, I will sell anything for money." Morgan then asked, "Well, what would you take?"

Carnegie thought that he now had $50,000 in his credit, and he said that he would take $60,000. The following morning John Morgan spoke to Carnegie once again and handed him two checks for $75,000. One was a $10,000 check, and the other check was for $60,000. Morgan spoke, saying, "Mr. Carnegie, you were mistaken. You sold out for $10,000 less than the statement showed to your credit. It now shows not fifty but sixty thousand to your credit, and the additional ten makes seventy."

Carnegie then held out the $10,000 check, offering it to Morgan. Carnegie said, "Well, that is something worthy of you. Will you please accept these ten thousand with my best wishes?" Morgan, being an honest man replied, "No, thank you, I cannot do that."

Carnegie has noted that it is this virtue of honor that keeps a business alive. What is more important than abiding by the laws is to be honorable.

From this point onward, Carnegie and the Morgans were dear friends.

In Carnegie's opinion, one must always be fair and honorable in business. He said that a business must be known not just for how it is legally righteous but that the managers, owners, and the people who run the business have a clean and respectable reputation not because they fear the law but because of their own virtue.

In his opinion, men who deal with stocks and wish to run a clean business can't do it.

After the incident with Union Pacific, Mr. Scott took up the project of building the Texas Pacific Railway. He called on Carnegie to meet with him in Philadelphia, which Carnegie did. He met with Mr. Scott and some of his friends, one of them being J.N. McCullough, who was at the time vice president of the Pennsylvania Railroad Company.

A loan had previously been secured for the Texas Pacific Railway but had not materialized and was applied for again by J.S. Morgan & Co. However, the only condition under which the bank would provide the loan was if Carnegie were to formally associate himself with those applying for the loan.

Carnegie did not want to do this and was then asked the hurtful question of whether or not he was willing to ruin his friends by not supporting them. Carnegie used all of his money for his manufacturing business. Furthermore, many people depended on him, such as his brother, his wife and his children, Mr. Henry Phipps, and Mr. Andrew Kloman.

Carnegie had already warned Mr. Scott against building such an important railway until he had a sufficient amount of money. He reminded Mr. Scott of his warning and said that such a long railway line could not be built if they were using temporary loans. Carnegie had previously paid $250,000 to be part of the venture, although he did not look favorably on the matter. He was not going to persuaded, however, to deliberately provide business for a manufacturing company that was not his and his partners' company.

Carnegie understood that he would not be able to pay back the loan from Morgan's bank at the end of sixty days or even his share of it. In addition, this was just one loan. For Mr. Scott and his partners to continue building the Texas Pacific Railway, they would have to get more loans, which was another headache.

The biggest difficulty for Carnegie was that this was yet another disagreement between him and Mr. Scott.

Soon after the meeting, Carnegie met with Mr. Scott and his friends in Philadelphia, but the meeting did not go well. Some of the most prestigious and promising men of the country were in great difficulty. Mr. Scott sustained great ridicule and humiliation but could only take so much. Due to his stress and state of mind, Mr. Scott died suddenly.

In Carnegie's opinion, Mr. Scott was easily affected.

As for some of the partners of Mr. Scott in the venture to build the Texas Pacific Railway, such as Mr. Baird and Mr. McManus, they too died prematurely. Both of them were not in the railway business, but like Carnegie, were in the business of manufacturing.

Carnegie said that if one is going to undertake a business venture, they should ask themselves these two questions: (1) would you be able to pay for all that might require your payment?, and (2) would you be willing to spend the money for a friend of yours that you support?

Carnegie said that if you could answer "yes" to both questions, then you could most definitely carry on with the venture. If you only answer "yes" to the first question, then you should think about immediately paying all that is required of you. If you have obtained a loan from a bank, the longer you don't pay off the loan, the longer you stay on their leash!

Once you clear the deck of all your debts and outstanding payments, you are free.

Although Carnegie refused to back the loan, he was called to come the following morning to New York with the people who were in the venture. Carnegie was happy to oblige. One other person had been called to join them, a Mr. Anthony Drexel. As the car drove on, Mr. McCullough said that he realized that all of the people in the car except for Carnegie were fools. He said that Carnegie had paid for all of his shares and did not have any debts whatsoever. He also said that all of them should have been as fortunate as he was.

Anthony Drexel then asked Carnegie to tell them how he had been able to believe that way. Carnegie responded by saying that he did so by not joining in something or attaching himself to something that he knew he could not pay when the time came. That was his principle. That kept him free of debt.

Sticking to this principle kept both Carnegie and his partners safe. They were all very strict about not involving themselves with large amounts of money that they could not pay back when called for. The only scenario in which they did this was when they were doing it for the benefit of their company.

While all this was happening, Carnegie regularly traveled to Europe, where he conducted talks for bonds' financial assets. In total, of all the negotiations Carnegie conducted on the continent, he had sold a total of $30 million. At the time, New York was not known as a financial center to those in London, for the Atlantic cable did not yet exist.

At this time, the bankers of London were also giving their balances to such places as Berlin, Paris, and Vienna instead of the United States. This allowed the banks to get a little more money from the interest rates. America was at the time thought to be not too safe for outside bankers wanting to make a profit by Europeans.

Carnegie was at full liberty to take several weeklong trips, and when he did he found himself not worrying about his business while he was away because Mr. Thomas Carnegie, his brother, and his friend Mr. Henry Phipps were taking care of the business very well indeed. He could trust them to look after the business while he was away.

Due to the financial success in negotiating with banks and getting them to buy securities and bonds, he was often given opportunities to enter the world of finance, although he declined. He preferred manufacturing more than he did dealing with money and stocks.

Carnegie thought more about making things and selling them rather than buying and selling pieces of paper. The money he made from his business, instead of investing it in other people, he invested in his own business, making it grow ever larger.

In the past, the Keystone Bridge Works had established workshops, which were rented out by other people. Furthermore, ten acres of land was acquired by Carnegie and his partners in Lawrenceville. They built several new shops there.

The Union Iron Mills was also perfected and improved, with more and more features being added. In the end, these add-ons and improvements made the Union Iron Mills the most prominent steel manufacturing concern in the United States.

Carnegie's business was prospering, and the profits he earned were reinvested in the business, used to buy new machinery, enlarge the business, build more mills and more land, and all that was necessary to expand the business.

Carnegie and his friends began building some rails for the Pennsylvania Railroad Company. More specifically, they were to build rails for the company in states to the west, but Carnegie soon pulled out of the venture. He followed the motto "Don't put all one's eggs in one basket." He thought that the proper way to go about things was to put everything into what you were doing and then always concentrate on that. He was not saying to confine yourself to just one line of work but to invest all your money in your business. He was also saying that if you are unable to invest your money in a business that will not grow and expand then you should invest your money in first-class bonds and shares so that you may receive a respectable profit. Furthermore, he was saying that to be successful you have to focus on your business and not be distracted by investing in others or running ten different businesses at once.

Carnegie's trip to Britain enabled him to meet authorities in the iron and steel manufacturing business. He was able to meet Bessemer, the creator of the Bessemer process; Sir Bernard Samuelson; Edward Martin; Sir Lothian Bell; Sir Windsor Richards; Evans; Bingley; and several other people.

Carnegie soon became a member of the council of the British Iron and Steel Institute and soon after that the president of the institution. He was the first president of the organization who was not British. This was something really grand indeed, and despite the glamor of being president of the British Iron and Steel Institute, Carnegie turned down the offer at first, fearing that he might not be able to serve the organization well enough because he lived in the United States.

Because Carnegie's bridge-building concern was using wrought iron to build its bridges and other things, Carnegie and his partners decided to get a blast furnace to make pig iron, the metal that is produced after being melted in a furnace. Pig iron is also known as crude iron.

Thus, in 1870, the Lucy Furnace, named after Carnegie's sister-in-law and the wife of his brother, the daughter of William Coleman, came into existence. If Carnegie and his partners understood the implications of getting a blast furnace for their business, they would put the matter off to a later time. Older manufacturers negatively viewed the expansion of Carnegie and his partners' business. Carnegie and his partners, however, did not care for negative mind-sets.

They believed that they would succeed by getting just one blast furnace.

Guesses were made for the cost of the blast furnace but only half of the real cost. Andrew Kloman did not know anything about blast furnaces, but this didn't matter, and no serious mistake or mishap occurred.

The Lucy Furnace was a big success. It performed better than Carnegie and his partners expected it to, and the furnace was melting one hundred tons of steel every day for one week, which had never happened before.

Carnegie and his partners' business was at the top of the list in terms of the number of products made every day, and many people came to watch what was being done.

Just because Carnegie and his partners had a blast furnace didn't mean their business would do well, and sometimes things did not turn out not as well as they hoped.

After the Civil War, the price of iron had decreased from ninety cents per pound to a mere three cents. Despite this drop, Carnegie and his partners' company was able to hold on. The financial manager of the business was always releasing the necessary money to solve pressing problems. Most troubling was the manufacture of pig iron in the workshops. Carnegie and his partners were able to make the acquaintance of one of the brothers who owned the company, Whitwell Brothers of England, a company that sold blast furnaces. Mr. Whitwell was able to advise Carnegie what to do, and after Carnegie and his partners incorporated his design, their furnace worked flawlessly. Whitwell was one of the visitors who came to see the Lucy Furnace, and Carnegie told him of the problem his business was facing. He replied by saying, "That comes from the angle of the bell being wrong." He went on to tell Carnegie how to fix the problem, but Kloman was unable to fully grasp what to do.

Carnegie said that two glass models of blast furnaces should be made and two bells as well. One of the models was to be a model of the Lucy Furnace, and the other model was to be a model of a blast furnace with the improvements that Mr. Whitwell had suggested. The two models were made, and experiments were conducted with both of them. What Whitwell had said was true. The Lucy Furnace's bell placed the large pieces of metal on the sides, and in the middle was a mass of metal that became extremely dense, which proved the metal was largely unaffected by the blast. As for Whitman's bell, the bell placed the pieces of iron in the center, which left only the surrounding part dense. This was what made the Lucy Furnace much more effective.

Carnegie has described Mr. Whitwell as a man who was cordially open with his knowledge and was not reserved simply because he might be giving away a secret ingredient. He very openly and willingly told Carnegie how to improve the Lucy Furnace, and thanks to him, Carnegie and his partners' steel business improved, with the Lucy Furnace performing much better. The Whitwell brothers became dear friends of Carnegie and remained so. This surviving Whitwell brother became the next president of the British Iron and Steel Institute after Carnegie.

Chapter 11 Carnegie's Steel Business

In 1870, chemistry was not at all related to steel—at least it wasn't thought to be. Unlike his fellow steel manufacturers, Carnegie decided to include the study of chemistry in his business, which resulted in even greater success. He has noted that the manager of the blast furnaces was always very rude and unrefined. He was a person who knew how to dole out punishments to set an example so that no one else would be a problem. He was also supposed to be able to miraculously find water or an oil well as how some people do with hazel rods.

The Lucy Furnace, the first blast furnace of Carnegie's steel company, did not work too well at first because there were several different types of limestone and ore. The furnace was always working with coke, which are the impure elements that are the by-product of heating steel. Finally, after the Lucy Furnace had experienced several problems, Carnegie and his partners decided to remedy the situation. The rough and clueless man who managed the furnace was dismissed, and a new man was put in charge. This gentleman was Henry M. Curry. He was a shipping clerk, but due to his impressive performance, Carnegie and his partners made him manager of the Lucy Furnace.

Mr. Henry Phipps, a friend of Carnegie, was the ultimate manager of the Lucy Furnace. He came to see the furnace every day and kept it working well. The Lucy Furnace was simply very large compared with other blast furnaces, which made it more prone to faltering.

Instead of attending church on Sunday mornings, Mr. Phipps went to see the furnace, while his sister and father went to Mass. Furthermore, if he were to go with his father and sister to church, his prayers would be about the Lucy Furnace!

After having appointed Mr. Curry to be manager of the Lucy Furnace, a chemist was hired to work with him. This chemist was Dr. Fricke, a German gentleman. Dr. Fricke enlightened Carnegie and his partners about several things. First of all, the iron sold by mines that were thought to be good were actually not. In reality, they had less iron than was believed. In contrast, the mines that were discredited and were not at all popular were really the ones with better ores. Thanks to Dr. Fricke and the use of chemistry, pig-iron manufacturing was able to flow smoothly in Carnegie and his partners' business.

When the Lucy Furnace once needed to produce an exceptional result for the good of the company, the ore that was going to be used was replaced by less impressive ore. This ore produced less than one-third the amount of iron of the superior ore. The error was caused because too much lime was used. In the end, nothing was gained.

Carnegie and his partners were in a far better position than their elder competitors. No steel manufacturer had ever engaged a chemist to work with them. They said they could not pay to have a chemist, but they were really worse off without one.

In the end, the Lucy Furnace was a good investment. It proved very profitable for Carnegie and his partners because they had chemistry on their side.

In 1872, Carnegie and his partners built a second blast furnace, now feeling that they knew how to properly use it. They also had more financial resources to use for the second furnace. In the past, several iron ore mines were not earning much and were not too popular, but they were having their goods purchased by Carnegie's company. On the other hand, the steel mines that were well known and said to produce good-quality ores did not have Carnegie's company as a customer.

One of the mines that Carnegie's company did purchase ore from was a mine called Pilot Knob in Missouri. The ore produced from this mine was very rich in silicon and had a low amount of phosphorus. Only a small amount could be used at a time so as to not damage the furnace. In truth, the ore was very valuable, and Carnegie and his partners bought large quantities of it. The owners of Pilot Knob were quite happy to have a good customer.

For some time, Carnegie and his firm were spending more money on eliminating the phosphoric cinders produced by the blast furnaces than it would have cost to buy pure cinder from other steel manufacturers. Every once in a while, a steel manufacturer had the bright idea to use his blast furnace to smelt flue cinder, but a blast furnace was not suitable for doing this work. Thus, the steel manufacturers of Pittsburgh were always discarding the cinders by throwing them into the river.

A steel-making company that an associate of Carnegie's Mr. Chisholm was working for was throwing their roll scale into the river, finding it utterly valueless. Carnegie then decided to obtain the roll scale. He contacted the son of a man who, among others, had come up with a method to obtain iron through a "direct process" as Carnegie described. The son agreed to do so, and he purchased the roll scale from the company Mr. Chisholm was working in for a mere half a dollar per ton! Carnegie was playing a joke on Mr. Chisholm, waiting for him to find out what was really happening. Unfortunately, Mr. Chisholm died prematurely and never realized Carnegie's joke.

After Mr. Chisholm's passing, those who assumed his position began to follow in the footsteps of Carnegie's steel manufacturing company.

Carnegie's time in the steel industry always showed him improving his business and reinvesting his money into it. Whenever his workers were not happy about something, Carnegie knew how to solve the issue, and they would be pleased.

Chapter 12 The Workers Strike

The workers at Carnegie's steel mill in Homestead led a strike, with the most prominent figure being a Mr. McLuckie, a splendid mechanic who worked at the mill. McLuckie was paid well, was married, and had a rather nice and comfortable life, but he still chose to support the strikers. As he had been given the position of burgomaster, he felt he could arrest the police officers who had come to the mill to keep everything peaceful. Everything was becoming worse and worse. McLuckie had even gone so far as to order that the police officers be murdered!

Carnegie was in the Highlands of Scotland at the time and only knew about the strike two days after it had begun. McLuckie would say several years later after everything was over that he believed that if Carnegie had been there everything would have been fine.

After the strike was put to an end, McLuckie had to flee from the authorities. He was charged with rioting, treason, murder, and several other crimes. He ran and hid and waited until everyone calmed down and forgot about what had happened. Aside from fleeing and hiding, his wife passed away, leaving him utterly alone. An associate of Carnegie's, the man who edited his autobiography, a John Van Dyke, bumped into McLuckie while he was trying to get a job at a mine that was fifteen miles away from the Mexican town of La Noria Verde. It was decided by all steel manufacturing concerns that they would not hire McLuckie, and thus he had decided to go to Mexico to find a job. Securing a position at the Mexican mine wasn't very easy, though, for the Mexicans wanted an inexperienced and ignorant person who would accept low wages.

After spending some time with McLuckie, Van Dyke wrote to Carnegie and said that he thought McLuckie had been treated unfairly. Carnegie replied and wrote with a pencil in the margin of the letter the following words, "Give McLuckie all the money he wants, but don't mention my name."

Van Dyke then contacted McLuckie and offered him some money, but McLuckie refused to accept, saying that he would make it on his own. Eventually, McLuckie was able to get a job as a well driver, and his life improved. He even remarried, marrying a Mexican lady. Finally, when all was better, Van Dyke told McLuckie the truth about the offer of money he had made sometime earlier. He said that it was Carnegie who had offered the money and not him. Surprised, McLuckie responded by saying, "Well, that was damned white of Andy, wasn't it?"

McLuckie really was appreciative of what Carnegie had done and even wrote a poem for him called "Just by The Way."

Another strike that took place involved the workers of the blast furnaces who worked producing steel rails. The workers had threatened to abandon the furnaces unless their salaries were raised to a higher amount by 4:00 on a Monday. In Carnegie's mind, if you make an agreement with someone and that person breaks or violates the agreement, there is no point in making another agreement with them. Despite his belief, Carnegie traveled from New York down to the striking workers to settle the matter. Once he was there, he called for the meeting of the blast furnace committee, the sole body that was leading the strike. He also called for the converting works and mill committees even though they were not involved in the strike. At the meeting, Carnegie spoke first to the leaders of the mill and converting works committees, asking them both whether or not they had an agreement with the company to work until the end of the year. Both answered in the affirmative. When Carnegie posed the same question to the leader of the blast furnace committee, Kelly, an Irishman, replied that he wasn't certain. A piece of paper was then passed around to all of the men seated, and they were to sign it. When it was Kelly's turn, he didn't go over what was on the paper and simply signed his name, not understanding what signing that piece of paper meant. Captain Jones, the manager, who was present at the meeting, immediately jumped up and censured Kelly for just signing the paper. Carnegie then said that he himself had signed many things that he did not fully read. He said that Kelly had been compelled to do so but went on to say that he should in the future read what he was about to sign for his own good. Carnegie went on to say that perhaps the blast furnace committee could continue their work for another four months and then properly go over the document they should sign if they wanted to renew their agreement. No one said anything to this proposition.

Carnegie then said, "Gentlemen of the Blast Furnace Committee, you have threatened our firm that you will break your agreement and that you will leave these blast furnaces unless you get a favorable answer to your threat by four o'clock today. It is not yet three, but your answer is ready. You may leave the blast furnaces. The grass will grow around them before we yield to your threat. The worst day that labor has ever seen in this world is that day in which it dishonors itself by breaking its agreement. You have your answer."

The members of the blast furnace committee then exited the room, and when Mr. Kelly reached the furnaces where the workers were waiting, he urged them to return to work. Carnegie was able to keep the blast furnace committee working, and all was well. Mr. Kelly even became an admirer of Carnegie from that moment forward.

The second strike involved the workers of the steel rail mills. They had sworn together that they would quit their jobs unless it was agreed they would be given higher salaries. That particular year was not too good for business, and even other steel manufacturers were decreasing the salaries of their workers. Because of this, Carnegie's company could not raise their workers' pay. Despite the low amount of revenue that the company was making, the workers of the steel rail mill in Pittsburgh still wanted higher salaries. If they were not going to be given higher pay, then they would abandon the mills.

Carnegie traveled to Pittsburgh to meet with the workers but was informed when he arrived that they were not there. The mills had been abandoned before the workers had originally planned to. The men had left and had decided to meet with Carnegie the following day. Carnegie said they could not meet him the following day for he would not be in Pittsburgh.

Carnegie then spoke to his partners and informed them that he was returning to New York.

Not long after the steel rail mill workers received Carnegie's message, they asked to meet with him in the afternoon before Carnegie left for New York. Carnegie welcomed their meeting.

When the workers came into his office, he told them that their leader, Mr. Bennett, said that Carnegie would take care of them. He went on to say that Mr. Bennett was correct and pointed out that Mr. Bennett had said that Carnegie was not able to fight. Carnegie corrected that by saying that he could, and that Mr. Bennett had not realized Carnegie was Scotch. Carnegie added that he would not fight his men, and the works would be started if two-thirds of the men voted in favor of starting the mills. The meeting came to an end.

Two weeks later Carnegie received a message at his house. The names of two workers in Carnegie's company and the name of a reverend were listed on the message. Carnegie asked his servant to check whether or not the two workers were among those who had shut down the furnaces before they were meant to do relative to an agreement. He was told that the two men were not among the workers who had violated the agreement with the company. Carnegie then said he would be glad to meet them.

During the meeting, the minister brought up the question of the striking workers. Carnegie then asked whether or not they had already voted and learned that they had not. Carnegie then said that he was not supposed to discuss this until the furnaces were restarted. Carnegie then showed them around New York.

The men soon returned to Pittsburgh, with nothing more said about the situation with the banked blast furnaces and the striking workers. The men had also now voted on the question of restarting or leaving the furnaces cold. The majority of the workers voted for restarting them. Carnegie thus traveled to Pittsburgh, where he presented to them the sliding scale for a second time. The sliding scale basically meant that the amount of money made from the the company's production determined the amount of money the workers received. This, in Carnegie's opinion, closely connected labor and money. When one prospered, the other did, and when one failed, the other shared the hardship.

In the end, the sliding scale was agreed to, and when everything was said and done, Mr. Bennett asked Carnegie for a favor. Carnegie responded by saying that he would agree to a reasonable request. Mr. Bennett then said that he wished for the "officers of the union," as he said it, to sign the agreement. Carnegie immediately agreed and asked for a favor in return. He asked that after the officers had signed the agreement the workers would too. He explained that if only the officers signed it the workers might feel upset with the decision of their superiors. A man standing next to Mr. Bennett then whispered in his ear, "By golly, the jig's up!" The "jig" really was up. Carnegie understood that if he did not grant Mr. Bennett his wish to allow the officers to sign the agreement it would have been used as an excuse for conflict between the men and the company.

That same sliding scale lasted for many years and was extremely successful among the workers.

Carnegie was often able to handle situations with style. He once had to meet with a certain group of men working for his company who had unreasonable requests. Carnegie had been told that a man who secretly ran a pub was dealing with these men.

He met with them and their leader, the owner of the secret bar. At the meeting, Carnegie was seated at one end of the table, while the leader of the workers making the demands was seated at the other. After Carnegie spoke to the other men around the table, suggesting a settlement, their leader prepared to leave and slowly put on his hat. Before he even got up, Carnegie spoke, "Sir, you are in the presence of gentlemen! Please be so good as to take your hat off or leave the room!"

No one said anything. It was clear that the man was in a tight spot. If he left the room, it would be considered rude, and if he stayed and removed his hat, he had been defeated by Carnegie. The man then removed his hat and placed it on the floor. He was completely silent for the rest of the meeting.

This showed that Carnegie knew how to deal with people. He knew how to control people by understanding how they behave and think, and he thus knew the right words to say to get someone to do something. In this case, he was speaking to a bully, as Carnegie called him. He knew how to force him to do something by putting him in a tight spot.

Chapter 13 Books & Marriage

With several friends, Carnegie took a trip around the world and wrote down his experiences, not at all intending for the book to become popular. The book was entitled *Round the World*. After being published, many distinguished people read and loved it. One of them said that he had never read any book but his ledger for several years, and that Carnegie's was the first he had ever read during those years. Another said that he had read the book from cover to cover. One said that he had not been able to sleep, having started the book and finished reading it at 2:00 the next morning. The book was very popular.

Just after 1885, Carnegie fell ill from typhoid fever. Several days before he left New York, he had not been feeling very well, and he became more ill after he returned. Doctors and nurses were called in to nurse him. Shortly after Carnegie fell ill, his mother did as well. At the same time, his brother, Thomas, also fell ill. While Carnegie was recovering, his brother and mother passed away. He was deeply affected when he found out. He felt alone and deeply shaken. It was as if he had been rocked to the core. This was when he got married. A friend of his, Louise Whitfield, would become his wife. She had already known Carnegie but said that she could not be with him for she had to care for her family. When Carnegie lost his family, he was also in need, and that is when Miss Whitfield turned her attention to Carnegie and married him. On April 22, 1887, the couple became husband and wife.

Carnegie has described his wife as a person who cared for all others and was a true "peace-maker," as he called her. He described his wife as the person who filled the gap in his heart after he lost his mother and brother. The pair were really very suitable for each other, with Louise taking care of him, and Mr. Carnegie feeling on top of the world with her by his side. She meant the world to him, and Carnegie said in his autobiography that he could not even begin to imagine a life without her.

Ten years after the couple married, on March 30, 1897, Margaret Carnegie was born. Louise had named their daughter after her husband's mother, and she asked for one thing from Carnegie. She said that now that they had a child they should be in a home where they could stay in peace—a home that was theirs. She meant that they should not always have to move but stay put. She said that their house should be in the Highlands of Scotland. Carnegie wholeheartedly agreed, and Skibo Castle was bought as the official home of the Carnegie family.

Living in the Highlands was really wonderful for him, as the cool, pure, and fresh air did him good.

Conclusion

After having made so much money from his business, Carnegie decided that it was time to distribute that wealth. When it was confirmed that he was going to retire, John Pierpont Morgan, son of Junius S. Morgan with whom Carnegie had previously dealt, bought Carnegie's steel company in 1901. Now a retired man, Carnegie lived the rest of his days giving to the public. He presented parks, libraries, university institutions, and funds to help thousands of people.

Pittencrief Glen, a wonderful place in Scotland according to Carnegie, was one of his many gifts to the public. His uncle, Bailie Morrison, had wanted to obtain for the town of Dunfermline a portion of the palace land in Dunfermline and the Dunfermline Abbey.

Carnegie's uncles, Morrison and Lauder, would later be the ones to lead a group of men to break down a specified wall. In the end, the Laird of

Pittencrieff declared that no Morrison was to be allowed into the Glen, and thus Carnegie was not allowed in.

When he grew up, however, he would be able to buy the Glen and become Laird of Pittencrieff himself. He would then proudly present Pittencrieff Glen to the public, a place where he hoped people would find peace.

One of the funds that Carnegie created was the Hero Fund. He had learned of an incident when the superior of a coal mine had sacrificed his life for the survival of the miners, and this inspired him to start the Hero Fund. The hero who had given his life had wanted to help in any way he could and lost his life in caring for them.

The Hero Fund was meant to provide financial support for the families left behind by heroes who sacrificed their lives to save others. Carnegie did not think that anyone would act as a hero simply for financial rewards. No. Carnegie believed that a true hero carried out heroic deeds not because he yearned for his reward but because he wanted to do good. If you ever do something *for* the reward, you are not a hero no matter how good or kind that act may be.

Carnegie also helped universities that were not doing too well at the time.

His acts of kindness and charity greatly benefited thousands of people in many ways. I will mention three: happiness, education, and money.

I truly hope you enjoyed learning about Carnegie. If so, I would be forever grateful if you could leave a review. Reviews are the best way to give feedback to authors and they also help your fellow readers find the books worth reading so make sure to help them out! Thanks in advance, I truly appreciate it.

p lol Quote

Made in the USA
Coppell, TX
18 November 2019